WHO TOLD YOU THAT?

DISCERNING TRUTH FROM LIE IN PROMINENT "CHRISTIAN" EXPRESSIONS

Savannah Sibert

ISBN 979-8-88851-818-2 (Paperback)
ISBN 979-8-88851-819-9 (Digital)

Copyright © 2023 Savannah Sibert
All rights reserved
First Edition

Scripture quotations marked CSB have been taken
from the Christian Standard Bible®, Copyright © 2017
by Holman Bible Publishers. Used by permission.
Christian Standard Bible® and CSB® are federally
registered trademarks of Holman Bible Publishers.

Scripture quotations are from The ESV® Bible (The
Holy Bible, English Standard Version®), copyright ©
2001 by Crossway, a publishing ministry of Good News
Publishers. Used by permission. All rights reserved.

All rights reserved. No part of this publication may be reproduced,
distributed, or transmitted in any form or by any means, including
photocopying, recording, or other electronic or mechanical
methods without the prior written permission of the publisher. For
permission requests, solicit the publisher via the address below.

Covenant Books
11661 Hwy 707
Murrells Inlet, SC 29576
www.covenantbooks.com

If you continue in my word, you really are my disciples. You will know the truth, and the truth will set you free.

—John 8:31–32 CSB

CONTENTS

INTRODUCTION

In John 8:44, we get a glimpse of Satan's true character. Jesus says that Satan was a murderer from the very beginning and that there is no truth in him. Jesus goes even further to call him the father of lies. Satan is a liar, but he is not a very creative liar. His schemes are simply counterfeits to what God offers. Unfortunately, our flesh is prone to believe his lies even though they are simply repetitions of the same ones he has uttered since the day he was cast out of heaven. We only must travel a few chapters into the very first book of the Bible, Genesis, to find proof of his deceitful character.

In Genesis chapter 3, we find Adam and Eve content in the garden in which God placed them. The garden was perfect. Sin had not yet entered the world, and the first humans were in perfect communion with the God who created them in His image and breathed life into them with His very breath. God gave them free reign and dominion over the entire garden and all the animals within it. They were free to eat from the bounty of every tree less one: the tree of knowledge of good and evil. The consequence of eating from that tree was death.

Satan comes to Eve in the form of a serpent. His first ploy is to plant doubt in her mind. In the very first verse of chapter 3, Satan asks, "Did God really say, 'You can't eat from any tree in the garden'?" Questioning the words God had spoken to them planted a small seed of doubt that created just enough room for compromise in Eve's mind. When Eve clarified what God had said about the fruit from the tree of knowledge of good and evil, Satan's next goal was to refute the truth in God's instructions.

In verses 4–5, Satan says, "No! You will not die. In fact, God knows that when you eat it your eyes will be opened and you will be like God, knowing good and evil." Eve had already accepted that compromise was a possibility, so when Satan spoke in a way that seemed true and fit with her fleshly desires, it became incredibly easy for her to justify disobeying God by eating the fruit. She ate of the tree, then she shared the fruit with her husband who, because of Eve's testimony, ate the fruit as well.

Sin is sticky, and it always reaches beyond yourself. Sin thrives on including others. The sins of Adam and Eve did, in fact, open their eyes. However, instead of making them like God, they saw that they were naked, felt ashamed, and began to make coverings for themselves. God warned them that eating from the tree would bring death, so why are Adam and Eve still alive? We must dig a little to find this answer, but in Romans 5:12–14, we learn that once Adam and Eve sinned, death came into the entire world because death is the consequence of sin. Before sin entered the picture, there would be no death, but because of their sin, now the world and its inhabitants are subject to the curse of death. Adam and Eve would not die instantly, but they would no longer live without ever facing a fleshly death.

Back to Genesis chapter 3, in verse 11, God comes to Adam and Eve, already knowing the full story, and asks, "Who told you that you were naked?" Three chapters into the Bible and we have the first example of how to weigh the things we hear. God asked Adam and Eve who they had been listening to, to remind them of what the truth of His voice had spoken to them before the serpent deceitfully opened his mouth. From the very beginning of creation, the Word of God has been the standard with which we are to separate truth from lies.

Sin entered humanity through a lie about what God said and a misconstruing of what He intended. As I mentioned in the very first paragraph, Satan has no new tricks. It's easy to think Satan's chief priority is to deceive the lost, or the people alive who haven't met and chosen to follow Jesus. Of course, Satan desires to keep anyone from an encounter with Jesus. However, let's look back at the story in Genesis. Adam and Eve had walked with and spoken with God. They intimately knew God, and yet Satan *still* came to them to attempt deception by discrediting God's word. Isn't it safe to say that we can expect those same sly deceptions to be directed toward us who walk with God today?

Jesus, Himself, was even tempted in this way. We find the account in Matthew chapter 4 of Satan boldly using scripture out of context to the Son of God in hopes that Jesus would fall to these same old tricks. If Jesus, in the flesh, was not spared from Satan's twisting of God's words as an attempt to deceive, you will not be spared from these kinds of attacks either. Jesus knew the Word because, as John chapter 1 tells us, He was the Word made flesh. He refuted Satan's claims by declaring the truth of what the word of God says.

One more lesson we should pay attention to in the account of Adam and Eve's fall is that Satan never had to speak directly to Adam; Eve's influence and false testimony was enough to convince Adam that the words Satan spoke were true and acceptable to act upon. We often give Satan credit that he isn't deserving of because, even today, his lies are being carried and repeated by people who follow Jesus. It may be unintentional; however, there is no denying that there are ideals, principles, and traditions being proclaimed and repeated by Christian men and women that completely go against the Word of God.

Why is this happening so easily? It's very simple. There are many people who proclaim Christ yet are not students of His Word. We have become content to sit in a church auditorium once or twice a week and allow our pastors and teachers to spoon-feed us perfectly packaged sermons. We accept every teaching as truth rather than comparing the messages we hear to the source of all truth, the Word of God.

If your pastor is not preaching directly from the Bible, is contradicting the Bible, or is not encouraging you to discover the truth held within it for yourself, it is time to move on and place yourself under the teachings of a new shepherd. I hope that you do feel a level of trust for your pastor, but it is so important to understand that we cannot rely on another person's studies of the Bible to hide the Word of God within our own hearts.

Another major factor is the ease of which information and aesthetically pleasing graphics loaded with out-of-context or completely incorrect words can be shared and digested on social media. We see a quote that resonates with us, and we share it with no regard for the truth or biblical soundness, or lack thereof, held within the words. Influencers and content creators can post a video conveying their own interpretations of a verse or a thirty-second clip from a forty-five-minute sermon that fits the narrative they endorse or want to push. Sources are very rarely checked, and that, friends, is incredibly dangerous ground.

We so easily ingest something that sounds good, and before we even realize it, we have allowed it to become doctrine that dictates our faith. This is evident even in the worship music genre as well. New music is constantly being pumped into the market faster than it has ever been before. Today, in churches all over the world, there are catchy, emotional worship songs being sung, and we have no clue if the words we are declaring even line up with what God says. If we, as those called out of darkness into the marvelous light of salvation, don't begin to eat, sleep, and breathe the living Word of God, we will continue to play into the deception that is wrapping tentacles around an entire world of people.

If we do not learn to first compare everything we read and hear to the truth of the Scripture, the enemy will use our lack of wisdom to begin slowly dragging away people, who once claimed faith in Jesus, under the guise of a "spiritual deconstruction." These theological or spiritual deconstructions more often than not bring their participants into a worldly reconstruction with ideals masquerading as enlightened holiness but truly leading them down the wide path of eternal destruction. This trend of "deconstruction" has also recently led to a massive exodus from the faith with people denouncing Jesus altogether.

The Bible proves over and over that humans easily get locked into religious traditions that become so sacred and dear they are willing to die for those traditions or to sacrifice others to protect them. Jesus addressed this very topic on a multitude of occasions with the Jewish leaders all throughout the Gospels. In Mark chapter 7, Jesus addresses the Pharisees and scribes regarding their man-made tradition and in verses 8–9, He says, "Abandoning the command of God, you hold on to human tradition. You have a fine way of invalidating God's command to set up your tradition!" So many times, we choose the tradition over the biblical truth. The truth from the Word of God will be offensive to our traditions if those traditions are found to be lacking when compared to Scripture.

It is past the time for followers of Jesus to evaluate the things they believe and proclaim. God's voice is still there asking us, "Who told you that?" He's not asking in preparation to condemn us; He's asking this question to draw our attention back to His Word. Devotions, blogs, and sermons can be excellent tools to assist us, but words written about the Bible are not where the power lies. That includes this book, the one you are currently reading, that I so passionately feel the Lord has called me to write. This book can be a tool to help you in your journey, but it is no substitute to the living, eternal Word of God. The power of God is discovered in His Word through the instruction, teaching, and counsel of the Holy Spirit.

In Luke chapter 10, Jesus is questioned by an expert in the law. These experts in the law studied, memorized, and knew the scriptures contained in the Old Testament books. The man asks Jesus how he can inherit eternal life. Jesus replies in verse 26, "What is written in the law? How do you read it?" Jesus was drawing this man back to the truth held within the Word of God just as God was drawing Adam and Eve back to His Word in the garden. It is just as important and powerful today as it was in the garden of Eden and when Jesus walked on earth with man.

Ephesians 6:17 tells us that the Word of God is our weapon against the spiritual warfare existing all around us. We cannot rely on a weapon we are unfamiliar with. We cannot fulfill our ministry in Christ without a devotion to Him though His Word. We cannot dispute or even recognize the lies of Satan without knowledge of the truth of the words of our God.

Scripture warns us to guard ourselves against the teachings of false prophets who will rise, especially in the last days, looking to deceive and distract from the truth. Colossians 2:8 says, "Be careful that no one takes you captive through philosophy and empty deceit based on human tradition, based on the elements of the world, rather than Christ." If we don't deeply know the truth of God's Word, how will we be able to accurately discern what is empty deceit and false teaching?

All scripture is inspired by God and is prof-
itable for teaching, for rebuking, for correcting,
for training in righteousness, so that the man of
God may be complete, equipped for every good
work. I solemnly charge you before God and
Christ Jesus, who is going to judge the living and
the dead, and because of his appearing and his
kingdom: Preach the word; be ready in season
and out of season; rebuke, correct, and encourage
with great patience and teaching. For the time
will come when people will not tolerate sound
doctrine, but according to their own desires, will
multiply teachers for themselves because they
have an itch to hear what they want to hear.
They will turn away from hearing the truth and
will turn aside to myths. But as for you, exercise
self-control in everything, endure hardship, do
the work of an evangelist, fulfill your ministry.
(2 Timothy 3:16–2 Timothy 4:5 CSB)

The Word of God is the standard to which every part of our lives should be compared. Our words carry weight in this world and culture that are filled to the brim with itching ears, especially if we are claiming that our words are endorsed by God. Just because a person begins a statement with, "God said..." or "I feel like the Lord wants me to tell you..." doesn't automatically make their words truth, but we can't decide what is truly from God if we are unfamiliar with His Word.

Satan would love for you to continue believing and holding onto false ideas about God. Holding on to these false ideas mini-mizes the authority and power you carry for the kingdom of God, but it also leads others into that same category in the exact way that

Eve's sinful actions encouraged Adam's disobedience. Everything we need to know and speak the truth is available and within reach!

The area I want to focus on in this book is just one part of allowing the Word to renew us, but I hope that through reading, you are charged and encouraged to begin the process of allowing God to renew every part of you in this same way. The remaining chapters of this book will be devoted to breaking down common phrases used by professing Christians today that have no biblical foundation or are based on an inaccurate view of the Scripture. My hope is that seeing popular quotes and ideals through the lens of the Bible will bring you into awareness of the places we have accepted Satan's small but impactful twists to the truth.

Each chapter will be dedicated to a specific quote or ideal. We will break down the meaning and typical use of it and then the problems with it. Then we can begin to dig in to find out what the Bible does have to say on the subject. As you read the following pages, you will find they are heavily saturated with scripture and examples from biblical accounts. I could expand greatly on what I think of each subject; however, my words can't hold a candle to the truth of God's Word. His Word is the final authority so that is where we will lean heavily. You will also find that some of the scriptures used are referenced in more than one chapter. I love how the Word can apply in so many different situations and discussions.

Another hope I have for this book is that through reading, you are encouraged to put in the work of breaking down the Scriptures for yourself. Don't rely solely on what I have written. Search out the verses listed on the following pages. Do your own studies on the topics we will address. God doesn't only explain His Word to the writers, worship leaders, and pastors. He wants the opportunity to teach all His children about His Word. He has things to teach you and things for you to share with those around you from His Word through the power of His Holy Spirit.

As you read, if you find yourself feeling shame or guilt that you believed something other than what the Bible says, please remember that growth is a beautiful part of a life of following Jesus. I, too, believed many of these ideas for years. God is so patient and kind with us as we walk through the process of sanctification. The truth of God's Word will set you free from false ideas, but it will also set you free from guilt and shame because, as Romans 8:1 encourages us, "therefore, there is now no condemnation for those in Christ Jesus, because the law of the Spirit of life in Christ has set you free from the law of sin and death." We do not have to understand everything at once when we submit to Jesus, but we are instructed to grow in maturity as we walk with Him. Hebrew 6:1 tells us that we must leave the elementary teaching and go on to maturity. There is grace for growth!

CHAPTER 1

GOD WILL NEVER GIVE YOU MORE
THAN YOU CAN HANDLE

We will jump right in with one of the more popular quotes that has been floating around the world of Christianity for many, many years. Some other variations include: "God won't allow you to walk through more than you can stand" and "God gives His toughest battles to His strongest soldiers." The attraction to this quote, and others like it, comes from experience with suffering and pain.

Bad things happen here on earth. People lose jobs, run short on money, face uncertainties in health, are mistreated by coworkers or family, and experience pain in many other ways. The belief that God will give us trials based on our personal level of strength is a very man-centered idea. We hate the trials, but we love the idea that God must see us as capable and incredibly strong to allow us to walk through these painful things. It's a boost to the precious ego to think that the God of the universe must be impressed with my strength, right?

Hearing that God won't give you more than you can handle is also extremely encouraging in situations where a person feels that they can't withstand another blow or tragedy. I have personally had this quoted to me in the middle of a long struggle with infertility. While the heart behind the statement was to encourage me, the encouragement did not line up with the Word of God. Anything that contradicts the Word of God is false, no matter how encouraging it sounds. This idea that God won't give us more than we can handle is not found anywhere in Scripture. In fact, there are more biblical examples to disprove this statement than there are to back it up.

> I have told you these things so that in me
> you may have peace. You will have suffering in
> this world. Be courageous! I have conquered the
> world. (John 16:33 CSB)

The first thing to note about this verse is that Jesus is the speaker. These statements were made in the presence of the men who were actively following Him, His disciples. This crowd included men like Peter, who followed Jesus to his death even after a brief lapse in devotion, and men like Judas, whose weaknesses led him to betrayal. Jesus never pointed out the strongest disciple to warn him of the trouble he would face because of his strength or assured the weaker disciples that they would face smaller trials. It was a blanket statement to all those following Jesus. Jesus wasn't giving them a heads-up that suffering could be a possibility; He was assuring them that suffering was an absolute in this life.

God's Word is eternal, so if it was true then for the disciples, it remains true for us today, as later confirmed in 2 Timothy 3:1, "But know this: Hard times will come in the last days." Prophetically speaking, we are in the last days. Whether Jesus returns in your lifetime or not, we are closer to His return than ever before and are seeing prophecies fulfilled at lightning speed that confirm this. This is a much deeper conversation than we will have here, but know this: hard times were assured for the disciples in Jesus's day, and they are assured for us in the current day.

Earlier in John chapter 15, Jesus tells the disciples to abide in Him. By abiding in and becoming one with Jesus, He warns that the world will hate them because they hated Him first. It is important to understand that when the world is spoken about in this context, it is referring to the worldly system of evil. The people who are hostile to or refuse God are the ones who will hate us because they are under the influence of Satan. Satan is an enemy to God, so any friend of God becomes an enemy to Satan as well.

From that, we see that the reason for the trials we face has a lot less to do with our own ability to withstand than it does with the One in whom we are abiding. Following Jesus will come with struggles. It is not a stretch or exaggeration to say that struggles are promised to us as followers of Jesus regardless of our mental or spiritual toughness. In fact, 1 Peter 4:12 tells us not to be surprised as if something strange is happening to us when we face trials.

As bleak as that news sounds, there is a bit of good news that comes with this knowledge. If the battles we face will come despite us, that means the victory in those trials isn't dependent on us either. Look back at John 16:33. Jesus says to have courage because *He has* conquered the world. My victory over struggles is reliant on Christ's victory only. To place my strength in the equation takes glory away from the Savior.

> But he said to me, "My grace is sufficient for you, for my power is perfected in weakness." Therefore, I will most gladly boast all the more about my weaknesses, so that Christ's power may reside in me. So I take pleasure in weaknesses, insults, hardships, persecutions, and in difficulties, for the sake of Christ. For when I am weak, then I am strong. (2 Corinthians 12:9–10 CSB)

In this letter to the church at Corinth, Paul presents a problem for the argument in favor of our first quote. If anyone could boast that the reason for their hardships or survival of those hardships was their own strength, Paul would be the one who could. Paul met Jesus in the middle of a life focused on persecuting Christians. His encounter with Jesus led to a radical life change. Paul, a Jewish Pharisee who was also a Roman citizen, left his life of affluence and influence to bring the gospel of Jesus to the world. His comfortable life before Jesus was completely turned upside down after encountering and choosing Jesus.

Paul was jailed, beaten, scorned, and rejected for the sake of his Savior, yet he persevered. Here in this letter, Paul is writing to his brothers and sisters in Christ with humility. Rather than hide his weaknesses, he talks openly about them because he is confident that it's his weaknesses that display the power of Christ rather than any strength he could muster.

Paul was a very strong servant of God, but he knew that the true secret to victory was the power of Christ. He knew that worldly strength is weakness when compared to the strength of God. The very weaknesses that made him unable to withstand persecution were the platform on which to demonstrate the miraculous way God's strength would sustain him.

If we jump backward to the first chapter in 2 Corinthians, we will find yet another statement by Paul that essentially destroys the validity of our quote. In verses 8 and 9, Paul writes this to the church of Corinth:

> We don't want you to be unaware, brothers and sisters, of our affliction that took place in Asia. We were completely overwhelmed—beyond our strength—so that we even despaired of life itself. Indeed, we felt that we had received the sentence of death, so that we would not trust in ourselves but in God who raises the dead.

They were completely overwhelmed *beyond* their own strength. So far beyond their strength that they literally believed death to be in their immediate future. Paul, and those with him, were admittedly given much more than they could handle; however, the weight of their despair reminded them to place their trust in the One who could handle it. Their survival was due to God's strength upholding them.

Paul ultimately did receive the sentence of death for his devotion to Jesus, as did many other disciples of Jesus. If God only allowed what a person could handle, there would be no one martyred for their faith; death is the ultimate example of experiencing more than

4

you are capable of withstanding. However, there have been people killed all over the world and more facing death even in current times because they refuse to denounce Jesus. Not only that, but strong, devoted followers of Jesus die every day, whether from battles with sickness, natural causes, tragic accidents, or any of a number of other causes. No one is strong enough to outrun the end of this earthly life.

Philippians 4:13 is one of the most quoted verses found within the Bible. It is the star of many tattoos, the substance of many social media status updates, and beautifully printed across many home decor pieces. It says, "I am able to do all things through him that strengthens me." This verse comes from another of Paul's letters, and it was written while Paul was under house arrest in Rome. Paul wasn't using this phrase flippantly or to encourage someone through taking a college final. Paul was encouraging the church that the strength of Jesus Christ was enough to sustain them through horrible circumstances such as unfair imprisonment, beatings, mocking, hunger, thirst, shipwrecks, and forced isolation, all of which, God had sustained or would sustain him through.

In one of the worst positions Paul could have ever pictured himself, a prisoner of the ruthless empire of Rome, he wanted the church to know that only the strength of Jesus was enough to continually pull him through. The book of Philippians is one of the most encouraging and joy-filled texts that was written by Paul, and he wrote it while locked away as a prisoner because of the very faith in Jesus he was writing so joyfully about. What a beautiful picture of the joy of the Lord as his strength.

Paul was once again living in a circumstance that was beyond what he could humanly stand, yet he was experiencing true joy. He kept ministering to the church because he was relying on the strength of the Lord rather than his own strength. It's all about God's strength. In every trial, season, or circumstance, our strength is not capable of handling much of anything, but God's is!

Paul could rejoice in his calamity because he had an accurate view of his true source. Think of a seed. The seed can't plant itself or choose the ground it would like to grow in. It relies on the hands of a knowledgeable gardener to tuck it away in the ground in the best place for its growth. The seed has no control over its survival; it can only do what its source of nutrients allows. A seed with access to enough water and sunlight can break through the ground and produce fruit. A seed with no steady source of nutrients will most likely shrivel and die.

Paul recognized that the only real source of strength is complete surrender to Christ. Complete surrender requires trust and reliance. Surrendering to and relying on Christ rather than himself removed all the heaviness of the burden Paul was bearing. His burden wasn't removed; he just found the necessary help to carry it for the duration of the trial.

Romans 5:3 says, "We also rejoice in our afflictions, because we know that affliction produces endurance, endurance produces proven character, and proven character produces hope." It's not our tolerance level that brings the struggles, but our endurance does come from persevering *through* our struggles. Each affliction provides the opportunity to endure for the sake of the gospel, and when you begin to realize the depth of your weakness, that is when the strength of God carries you through the fire.

Another example of a person suffering greatly at the hands of Satan is the account of Job, found in the Old Testament book of Job. Job was faithful to God and was known for abiding in God. Satan saw the way God blessed Job and desired to test him, so God allowed it. Satan killed Job's children, killed his flocks and servants, and attacked his health. Job lamented before the Lord and regretted the day that he was even born because of the suffering he was enduring. Job wanted to die.

I would be willing to bet that Job would argue he had been handed much more than he, by himself, was able to handle. In Job 2:13, we learn that Job's suffering was so intense his friends came and sat on the ground with him for seven days without speaking a word. Job's grief must have been unfathomable for these friends to be left speechless for so long. Though Job grieved, questioned, and suffered through the trial, he ultimately remained faithful to God.

Job had history with God and was able to look back on who he had known God to be all his life. He drew strength from the fact that

WHO TOLD YOU THAT?

God was the one who gives and takes away, and God, alone, was in control. In Job 2:10, after Job's wife told him to curse God and die, Job says, "Should we accept only good from God and not adversity?" Just like Jesus explained to His disciples, Job's devotion to God and Satan's hatred of God brought the attention of Satan and his testing, not Job's strength.

One of the most incredible parts of Job's story to me is found in the end of his account. In chapters 38–41, after Job had survived and wrestled through calamity, despair, and heartbreak, God speaks to Job from a whirlwind. God reminds him in great detail of His power, authority, and might. Job says in verses 5–6 of chapter 42, "I had heard reports about you, but now my eyes have seen you. Therefore, I reject my words and am sorry for them; I am dust and ashes." Through his suffering, He was able to see God rightly. Seeing God rightly will always lead us to humility and repentance.

One specific verse is often quoted in an attempt to prove the validity of our featured quote, so we must address it as well. First Corinthians 10:13 says, "No temptation has come upon you except what is common to humanity. But God is faithful; he will not allow you to be tempted beyond what you are able, but with the temptation he will also provide a way out so that you may be able to bear it." In this verse, Paul is not addressing suffering or trials at all, contrary to popular belief. Paul is referring to the temptation to sin. When we understand this difference, this verse takes on an entirely new meaning.

In the beginning of this chapter, Paul is reminding the church of Corinth of the lessons that can be learned from Israel's past. The people of Israel witnessed many miraculous displays of God's power yet fell time and time again to sin. Some of their sins that Paul lists here are idolatry, sexual immorality, testing Christ, and complaining.

He specifies in verse 11 that these struggles the Israelites faced and the sins they took part in were recorded for our instruction. After saying that God won't allow us to be tempted beyond what we can handle, Paul immediately warns in verse 14 to flee from idolatry. Paul understood that human nature makes us very prone to be tempted to worship other things above God, also known as idolatry.

His warning in these verses was to make us aware that idolizing anything above God is a sin and that no one is completely safe from that temptation. Fortunately, God understands our weaknesses. He knows each of His children deeply and intimately, so He knows your limits on withstanding temptation. Keep in mind that temptation comes from Satan, not God. We discussed examples of this in the introductory chapter, and you can also find more on temptation in James chapter 1.

Notice, however, that our verse in 1 Corinthians doesn't say that God will abolish the temptation altogether when He sees that it's too much for a person to bear. The Word tells us that God will provide a way out. This means that in the middle of temptation, God will provide a way for you to operate in His strength and remove yourself from the circumstance that is causing you to be tempted.

Jesus tells His disciples in Matthew 26:41 to watch and pray so they wouldn't fall into temptation. Hebrews 2:18 tells us that Jesus suffered when tempted and so is able to help those who are being tempted. Jesus wouldn't need to help us through temptation if we were only given what our fleshly strength could handle. Our victory through temptation comes from yielding to God and abiding in His power.

I would argue that it actually takes more strength to leave temptation than it does to continue in it or to give in to it. So Jesus helping us while being tempted is Him giving us the strength to remove ourselves from the situation that is causing the temptation. His Word hidden within your heart and His Spirit dwelling within you will provide the strength you need to take the exit God provides.

> Do you not know? Have you not heard?
> The Lord is an everlasting God, the Creator
> of the whole earth. He never becomes faint or
> weary; there is no limit to His understanding.
> He gives strength to the faint and strengthens the
> powerless. Youths may become faint and weary,
> and young men stumble and fall, but those who
> trust in the Lord will renew their strength; they

will soar on wings of eagles; they will run and not become weary, they will walk and not faint. (Isaiah 40:28–31 CSB)

I will become weak and weary in the middle of a trial that seems to have no reprieve; God will not. I will lose strength when tempted; only God can renew that strength. My fleshly power will dwindle based on my circumstances because I am flesh. God is not flesh. He is the beginning and end, the Alpha and Omega, the One who was and is and is to come. His power cannot be limited or lessened, and He's made that power available to you and me through the blood of Jesus, the help of the Holy Spirit, and His eternal Word.

Knowing now that God may, in fact, allow us to walk through much more than our flesh can handle, what can we do to prepare ourselves for these times of struggle and hardship? Paul gives this charge in Ephesians 6:11–18:

> Put on the full armor of God so that you can stand against the schemes of the devil. For our struggle is not against flesh and blood, but against the rulers, against the authorities, against the cosmic powers of this darkness, against evil, spiritual forces in the heavens. For this reason take up the full armor of God, so that you may be able to resist in the evil day, and having prepared everything, to take your stand. Stand, therefore, with truth like a belt around your waist, righteousness like armor on your chest, and your feet sandaled with readiness for the gospel of peace. In every situation take up the shield of faith with which you can extinguish all the flaming arrows of the evil one. Take the helmet of salvation and the sword of the Spirit—which is the word of God. Pray at all times in the Spirit with every prayer and request, and stay alert with all perseverance and intercession for all the saints.

Not one piece of the armor prescribed for the battle is attainable without yielding to God. These pieces of armor rely solely on God. His truth is your belt, His Word is your sword, and prayer is your lifeline. Even your feet are to be sandaled with readiness for His Word. You will survive the hard times by daily surrender to God. Your victory will come from arming yourself with His Word and resting in His power alone. In the same way, Paul was confident that God's grace was sufficient to sustain him in every struggle, you can be confident of God's grace in every aspect of your life as well.

It was never God's intention for you to struggle through in your own power. God is a loving and personal God. In 1 Peter 5:7, we are invited to cast all our anxieties on God because He cares for us. Jesus says in Matthew 11:28–30, "Come to me, all you who are weary and burdened, and I will give you rest. Take up my yoke and learn from me, because I am lowly and humble in heart, and you will find rest for your souls. For my yoke is easy and my burden is light." Psalm 55:22 says, "Cast your burden on the Lord, and he will sustain you; he will never allow the righteous to be shaken." Even in the pages of the Old Testament, you can find reminder after reminder of God's provision for His people through trials.

In 2 Corinthians chapter 1, before Paul tells of their great affliction and despair in Asia, he reminds us that God is the father of mercies and the God of comfort. God comforts us during these trials and then empowers us to comfort others who are walking through hard things. God strengthens us so that we, in turn, can encourage and strengthen our brothers and sisters with His Word and our testimonies through the power of the Holy Spirit living within us. Even our pain is not without purpose.

So yes, you will walk through more than you can handle. Take heart and stand firm because you are not expected to rely on your own meager strength, as the psalmist recounts Israel's victory in praise to God in Psalm 44:3: "For they did not take the land by their sword—their arm did not bring them victory—but by your right hand, your arm, and the light of your face, because you were favorable toward them." The God who called you from death to life is more than capable to handle whatever storm you find standing at your door.

With Paul being a major source for this chapter, it is only fitting to close it out with his encouragement to the church in Romans 8:18. He writes, "For I consider that the sufferings of this present time are not worth comparing to the glory that is going to be revealed to us." As you face the struggles of life, remember that this life is not your permanent placement. If you have been redeemed by Jesus, you have the promise of eternity with Him. He will sustain you until His glory is revealed to you in eternity.

CHAPTER 2

THE ENEMY HAS TO FLEE AT THE
MENTION OF THE NAME OF JESUS

Just reading this phrase, I'm sure a string of popular worship song lyrics ran through your brain. This idea of being able to simply speak the name of Jesus and drive away any fear, evil, or darkness around us is intriguing. I believed this one for many years and even sang it as a declaration many times. I believed it so deeply that I remember lying wide awake in my bed one night, angry with God because I had spoken His name and still felt no relief from the fear that was plaguing my mind. When the Lord lovingly prompted me to locate the scripture that confirmed this idea, I was completely shocked to find that it is not anywhere in our Bible.

The Bible speaks endlessly of the power of God and the power of Jesus. Many verses mention the power of their names as well. God's name is described as a strong tower in Proverbs 18:10. Philippians 2:9–11 tells us Jesus was given the name above every name, and that ultimately, every knee will bow at the name of Jesus. Yet nowhere does the Scripture say that the enemy must flee when we simply mention the name of Jesus. I'm afraid that the overuse of this phrase has duped an entire generation of people into believing they can walk into a spiritual battle, say "Jesus" out loud, and it's suddenly a spiritual safe zone.

This is not only bad theology, but dangerous theology for followers of Jesus because spiritual warfare is very real. Demons are real.

Satan is real. The spiritual realm where they reside is incredibly real and active. Ephesians 6:12 teaches us that our battle is not against flesh and blood but against the rulers and spiritual powers of darkness. 1 Peter 5:8 warns about being alert and sober-minded because "your adversary the devil is prowling around like a roaring lion, looking for anyone he can devour." We are spiritual beings residing in fleshly bodies temporarily, and it is imperative that we understand where the true power is in facing spiritual enemies and their attacks.

Not only is this phrase not mentioned in the Bible, but if we take a deeper look into what the Bible does say about Satan and his demons and the way Jesus cast them out, we find many examples of scripture that contradict this phrase as well. One major defense I've heard in favor of the validity of this quote is that Jesus commanded His disciples, and in turn commanded us, to cast out demons and heal in His name. This is accurate; you'll find a multitude of examples of this all throughout the New Testament. However, a deeper dive into the way Jesus did these things tells a much bigger story.

In Mark chapter 1 verses 21–27, we find Jesus and His disciples in a synagogue in Capernaum. The people in attendance are already amazed at Jesus because the authority in His way of teaching is different from anything they had ever heard. A man enters the synagogue who is possessed by a demon. The demon cries out from within the man in verse 24, "What do you have to do with us, Jesus of Nazareth? Have you come to destroy us? I know who you are—the Holy One of God!" This demon not only recognizes that Jesus is the Son of God, but in his outcry, he says the name of Jesus as well. If the name of Jesus alone is supposed to drive out demons, how could this demon *speak* His name and remain exactly where he was?

Jesus replies, "Be silent, and come out of him!" At the command of Jesus, the demon left the man. It wasn't the name of Jesus that caused the demon to vacate the property—Jesus never mentioned His own name—it was the authority of Jesus that rebuked this unclean spirit. In Matthew 28:18, Jesus tells His disciples that He has been given all authority in heaven and on earth. In Mark 3:14, Jesus tells them that He has given them authority to have power over the enemy. After that, the disciples began casting out demons with that authority as well. The authority of Jesus was the difference maker, and that is still where things start to shift in the spiritual realm!

After Jesus's death and resurrection, the disciples began to minister with great boldness. People took notice of the way they commanded demons to leave and people to be healed in the name of this Jesus. In Acts 19:11–20, we see a group of exorcists who decided they would use this name to cast out demons on their own. These exorcists saw things happen in the spiritual realm when the disciples used the name of Jesus and assumed that it was a kind of secret code word that could be used to empty the air of evil. In verse 13, they spoke to some demon-afflicted people, saying, "I command you by the Jesus that Paul preaches!" The evil spirit replies, "I know Jesus, and I recognize Paul—but who are you?"

This demon knew exactly who Jesus was. Don't miss that it was also able to say the name of Jesus and remain within its host. It recognized Paul because Paul followed Jesus and carried His authority. These men, however, didn't know or follow Jesus. They only had knowledge *about* Jesus, so they had no access to the authority of Jesus.

Many people have knowledge about Jesus. There are historical accounts of Jesus outside the Bible that recognize Him as a prominent teacher or even a prophet. On the contrary, there are accounts that call Him a fraud and a heretic. Millions of people know His name or a few things He did while on earth with that being the extent of their knowledge. Many of the people in that category would go as far to say that they believe that God is real and that Jesus is His Son.

James 2:19 tells us that even the demons believe, and they tremble or shudder at the thought. The demons in our last examples knew exactly who Jesus was. They never attempted to dispute Him as the Son of God or the Messiah. In Mark 2:7–12, as Jesus was ministering, the text tells us in verse 11 that when unclean spirits saw Him, they would fall down before Him and proclaim that He was the Son of God. Even as He was walking in a fleshly body, evil had no choice but to respond to His presence and obey His commands. Knowing about Jesus is a good place to start, but truly knowing Jesus as Savior and Lord is where the transformation of our lives comes, and with that, His authority as well.

Think of it like this: you receive a handwritten letter from a stranger who has no affiliation with your mortgage lender, but the letter they send you says that your house now belongs to them. They have no authority to take your house for themselves, so you pay no attention to the letter this seemingly delusional person sent you. If, however, you receive the same letter from your bank or from a specific employee of your bank with the official heading and signatures, you would take the typed or written words much more seriously. The bank has authority to claim your home because they financed the sale. You would respond to the letter that came with authority immediately just like the enemy has no choice but to respond to the authority of the Lamb of God. The name of Jesus is nothing without the authority that comes with the person of Jesus.

In Mark 7:24–29, Jesus is approached by a woman. A woman gathering the courage to speak to a Jewish man was not an easy feat alone, but this woman was also a Gentile. She would've been looked down upon by most Jews for both. The woman had a daughter who was afflicted by a demon, and she came to Jesus looking for healing for her little girl. Jesus did, in fact, cast out the demon. He never physically visited the girl or spoke audibly to the demon afflicting her. His authority reaches even beyond words and beyond this physical realm of earth.

Another biblical example of the authority of Jesus can be found in Mark 4:35–41. Jesus and His disciples had all boarded a boat to cross the Sea of Galilee. The terrain around this sea makes it very prone to windstorms that can bring extremely large waves. On this night, one of those windstorms arose. The Bible tells us that the waves were breaking over the side of their vessel, swamping the inside of the boat with water. The disciples were terrified, and Jesus was asleep.

> So they woke him up and said to him,
> "Teacher! Don't you care that we're going to die?"
> He got up, rebuked the wind, and said to the sea,
> "Silence! Be Still!" The wind ceased, and there

was a great calm. Then he said to them, "Why are you afraid? Do you still have no faith?" And they were terrified and asked one another, "Who then is this? Even the wind and sea obey him!" (Mark 4:38–41 CSB)

The disciples had seen Jesus drive out demons before this moment. They had been there to witness firsthand as He healed diseases and injuries. They had even watched Him pronounce people as clean, which typically required certain requirements to be met, a sacrificial offering, and the approval of the anointed priest. Greater still, they had witnessed Him forgive sin, which was unheard of. Yet watching the wind and sea obey His voice, they were amazed that even nature bowed to the authority of their Teacher. This is the same authority that Jesus places in us as His followers even today.

How do we know that Jesus has placed His authority in those who follow Him today? John 14:12 says this: "Truly I tell you, the one who believes in me will also do the works that I do. And he will do even greater works than these, because I am going to the Father." Then later in verses 16 and 17, He says, "And I will ask the Father, and he will give you another Counselor to be with you forever. He is the Spirit of truth." He also clarifies that the world can't receive the Holy Spirit because it doesn't see or know Him, but He will remain in and be with followers of Jesus.

Peter also spoke about the Holy Spirit in Acts chapter 2 after he and the disciples received the Holy Spirit for themselves on the day of Pentecost. Peter stood up to speak to the crowds in Jerusalem about Jesus and call them to repentance. In verse 38, Peter says, "Repent and be baptized, each of you, in the name of Jesus Christ for the forgiveness of sins, and you will receive the gift of the Holy Spirit." The Holy Spirit is given when we receive the salvation of Jesus through repentance. Peter's sermon proves that the Holy Spirit didn't end with the first disciples who received Him.

In 1 Corinthians chapter 6, Paul is speaking to fellow believers about the importance of glorifying God with their bodies. He was warning against sexual immorality, and while that seems to be very much off the topic for this chapter, the reason Paul gives puts a great deal into perspective for us when speaking of the assurance that the Holy Spirit is placed within followers of Jesus. In verse 19, he says, "Don't you know that your body is a temple of the Holy Spirit who is in you, whom you have from God?" Earlier in chapter 3, Paul writes in verse 16, "Don't you yourselves know that you are God's temple and that the Spirit of God lives in you?"

While this terminology could be confusing to us today, the people of that time period would've marveled at this description. Temples were well known and frequently visited. Each secular religion boasted their own grand temples for their respective gods, but more importantly, the Jewish people had worshipped at a tent, then a tabernacle, and finally a temple since their days in the wilderness. God's glory and presence dwelt within the temple. The temple is where sacrifices were made for sin and forgiveness of that sin was available.

Inside the temple, in the most holy part of the sanctuary sat the Ark of the Covenant, which housed the mercy seat where God's presence and glory was. The anointed priest was the only person allowed to enter into that holy place and would die if he were found to be carrying any sin or approaching the Lord's presence without taking the prescribed steps beforehand. God's presence inside that temple was a big deal. The temple no longer stands in Jerusalem, but even today, hundreds of people flock daily to the Western Wall and the remnants of the temple mount to bring their petitions and worship.

What Paul was saying to the Corinthians is that the same presence of God that dwelled inside the holy temple then now dwells within God's people through the Holy Spirit. Our God no longer dwells in man-made temples but within His children. It is an honor to carry the Spirit of God within us! Jesus's death and resurrection made it possible for us to house the Spirit of God and because of that, His authority as well.

The Holy Spirit is the Spirit of God, and the Holy Spirit is who will empower us to do the things that Jesus did. Jesus tells the disciples in Acts chapter 1 that they will receive power when the Holy Spirit comes upon them. In John 16:7, Jesus tells the disciples, who didn't want to think about losing their teacher, that it was to their advantage that He went away because He had to leave them for the Holy Spirit to be sent to them. The Holy Spirit is a seal on followers of Jesus, and He gives His power and authority through the Spirit.

This is incredible news for us. We can walk in power because our Savior first walked in power and His sacrifice on the cross brings us into unity with the Father through the blood of Jesus and the Holy Spirit. That power includes authority over the enemy and yes, even the demons. Jesus does give a warning with this knowledge in Luke 10:20 as the disciples were marveling that even the demons obeyed them in Jesus's name. He says, "However, don't rejoice that the spirits submit to you, but rejoice that your names are written in heaven." It is an honor to carry the authority of Jesus, but the biggest honor of all is to be saved by the blood of a perfect Savior.

All the authority in the world cannot compare to the gift of being called sons and daughters of the living God. We can get so focused on the enemy that it distracts us from the victory Christ already purchased and won on the cross. Casting out demons and healing are still active gifts in our faith; however, whether we receive or are part of a miracle like that on earth or not, we must keep in mind that every person we meet is guaranteed to stand before the Lord one day in eternity. Our primary focus as children of God should be to love like Jesus and bring people into the knowledge of the gospel. Miracles may very well be a part of that, but the greatest miracle is the miracle of salvation through Jesus.

James 4:7 tells us, "Therefore, submit to God. Resist the devil, and he will flee from you." Order matters in the kingdom of God. To have the strength to resist the devil and cause him to flee, we must first submit to the authority and power of God. Satan's fleeing has much less to do with me than it does with the God who lives inside me. Submitting to God through repentance and receiving His gifts of mercy and salvation is the beginning of everything, not the last step to secure eternal life. When we truly submit to God, He gives us the strength to resist the devil.

One more section of text we need to examine is Matthew 7:21–23. Jesus is teaching here as part of the "Sermon on the Mount."

He warns that not everyone who has called on His name will enter heaven but only those who do the will of the Father. In verse 22, He says that many will say to Him, "Lord, Lord, didn't we prophesy in your name, drive out demons in your name, and do many miracles in your name?" Jesus's response to these people is one of the most chilling sentences in the Bible. He says, "I never knew you. Depart from me, you lawbreakers."

How can this be? These people successfully used the name of Jesus to perform miracles, yet Jesus tells them He *never* knew them. The text doesn't say that Jesus once knew them and they fell away from the faith. It is clear that they never surrendered and submitted to God through the salvation of Jesus. Rather than being in Christ, they were in the world. With that being said, we know they could not carry His Spirit or authority because the world cannot receive the Holy Spirit.

We have to remember that demons are employed and commanded by Satan. Satan will not do anything that brings glory to God. He will, however, do what he can to provide a counterfeit to the truth of God. Satan does have authority over his demons. It is most likely the case that these people were swayed by false prophets who sold them on a counterfeit faith that had the appearance of truth and holiness yet was a teaching of Satan. These people could have been under the impression that they were commanding the spiritual realm in the power of God, yet the only power at work in these cases was the evil, deceptive power of Satan.

This isn't the only example we have of Satan empowering people to perform miracles. In Exodus chapter 4, God is preparing Moses to go before Pharaoh and plead the case for Israel's release from Egyptian captivity. He empowers Moses and his brother Aaron to perform signs because Moses is afraid that Pharaoh won't believe that they were truly sent by God. As Moses and Aaron present the message before Pharaoh in chapter 7, Pharaoh demands a sign. Aaron throws down his staff as God instructed him to, and it becomes a serpent.

In verse 11, the Bible tells us that Pharaoh called his sorcerers to join them. They each threw down their staves, and each staff became a serpent as well. However, to prove God has the ultimate authority, the serpent that came from Aaron's staff swallowed up all the other serpents. The Bible says these sorcerers were able to do this sign by their occult practices. Based on what is known from Egyptian history, Egypt worshipped many gods, and the sorcerers here were claiming power from these gods. However, we know from Psalm 135:15–17 that every other god is an idol who cannot see, speak, or hear. The power these sorcerers were working through was the power of Satan.

Second Thessalonians chapter 2 warns of the coming of the Antichrist in the last days. When the Antichrist comes, he will claim to be God and even sit in the yet-to-be-built third temple, demanding worship. Verse 9 says, "The coming of the lawless one is based on Satan's working, with all kinds of false miracles, signs, wonders, and with every wicked deception among those who are perishing." He will display power, but the Word is clear that every part of his time on earth is based on Satan's working.

I want to add a reminder here of the importance of being grounded in the Word of God. The spirit of the Antichrist is alive and working. As we inch closer and closer to Jesus's return, false prophets with false gospels will rise and will attempt to sway anyone they can. You can resist the lies by knowing God and His true character through His Word. Please don't take this as a reason to be fearful; only let it spur you on to be prepared and ready to stand firm on the truth. God wants you to be able to pick out truth from lie, and He will help you do so!

It is also a possibility that these people were a part of a church or group of people that *was* empowered by the Holy Spirit to perform these signs and miracles. You've probably all heard the phrase *guilty by association*. That phrase does not apply here. Being in attendance when a person exercises their God-given authority over demons does not automatically add that credit to your account as well. Salvation and surrender to God through Jesus are personal. Repentance is personal. Truly following Jesus is a choice that must be made for each individual person.

Jesus said that not every person who simply calls on His name will enter heaven. Jesus is not saying that true salvation is unpredictable or unreliable. True salvation leads to eternity with Jesus, but it must be true repentance. Calling on Jesus's name without turning away from sin is not salvation. It begins with a decision in the heart and is followed by surrender to the will of God.

> Peace I leave with you. My peace I give to you. I do not give to you as the world gives. Don't let your hearts be troubled or fearful. (John 14:27 CSB)

I mentioned in the beginning of this chapter that a struggle with fear was what led me to further investigate this topic. We discussed a great deal about demons and the enemy in the previous paragraphs, but I know that fear is such a plague in our culture today. I would be willing to bet that most of you reading have struggled, like me, with deeply rooted fear in the past or find yourself struggling with it now. How do we combat fear in our daily lives if it isn't by just saying the name of Jesus?

Let's start by looking into what the Bible says about fear. Fear is not from God, nor is it a part of God. Most of the verses you'll find in the Bible that specifically mention fear are instructing us not to fear or encouraging us that there is no reason to fear with God as our salvation and hope. It would be disheartening if that were all it said on the matter. Fortunately for us, the Bible has a lot to say about the peace that comes from God, and the peace that God gives is the remedy to our fleshly fear.

In Isaiah 26:3, we learn that God will keep the mind that is fixed on Him in perfect peace. Earlier in Isaiah chapter 9:6, in a prophecy about Jesus being born in the flesh, He is given the name Prince of Peace. Colossians 3:15 tells us that we're called to the peace of Christ. Peace is a part of our Father and Savior as well as a promised part of a life following Jesus.

> For God has not given us a spirit of fear, but one of power, love, and sound judgement. (2 Timothy 1:7 CSB)

If you have given your life to Jesus, you have been given the Holy Spirit, as we discussed previously. The Holy Spirit is not a Spirit of fear and is not associated with fear. The Spirit that dwells within you is a Spirit of power, love, and a sound mind. One of the fruits of the Spirit, which we read about in Galatians chapter 5, is peace. Romans 8:6 says, "Now the mind-set of the flesh is death, but the mind-set of the Spirit is life and peace. Romans 8:15 describes it this way, "For you did not receive a spirit of slavery to fall back into fear. Instead, you received the Spirit of adoption, by whom we cry out, 'Abba, Father!'" Those who are led by the Spirit of God are sons and daughters of God, and His children have access to His perfect peace!

In Ephesians chapter 6, God's Word is described as the gospel of peace. In Psalm 119:165, the psalmist writes, "Abundant peace belongs to those who love your instruction; nothing makes them stumble." Once again, we see the Word of God and the Spirit of God working together to provide what we need.

If fear is not given by God, then we must deduce that it is an evil attack of Satan and his demons. We already know that demonic forces must obey the authority of Jesus. Remember that the authority of Jesus is placed within us through the Spirit, and just like the enemy, fear has no choice but to submit to that authority. The Spirit teaches us and brings us into understanding of the Word, which is a part of God, and brings us peace as well.

There is some confusion about fear when it comes to God because you will find verses that instruct us to fear God or encourage that the fear of the Lord is a good thing. This fear is not the same as fear that comes from the enemy. The fear we should have of God is a reverence and awe of God. Fearing God is recognizing His power and authority. This type of fear, or respect, is beneficial, as it allows us to see God and His power rightly. For those of us who are saved, this does not mean we should be terrified of God.

And whatever you do, in word or deed,
do everything in the name of the Lord Jesus,
giving thanks to God the Father through him.
(Colossians 3:17 CSB)

Please don't take from this chapter that we don't have to say the name of Jesus, because our personal authority is enough on its own. We should absolutely be praying in the name of Jesus. We should command the enemy to leave in the name of Jesus. We should be teaching people to call on His name because the name of the Lord is a strong tower, and the righteous can run to it and be saved. Acts 4:12 tells us that the name of Jesus is the only name by which we can receive salvation. We should be making disciples and baptizing them in His name. Jesus's name is powerful because the person of Jesus is powerful.

The main point of this chapter is to gain an understanding that the authority in His name is much more than a secret password for us. We must keep in mind that truly praying in the name of Jesus means bringing our own hearts in line with the will of God instead of the other way around. Praying in Jesus's name is a declaration that you are coming into alignment with the will and authority of Jesus, not declaring that God will come into alignment with yours.

God's will is perfect, and His plans have no fault. We should come into prayer, asking God to put His desires in our hearts and give us the perspective of heaven and then pray in accordance with that even when those desires differ drastically from our own. Sticking the name of Jesus on the end of a prayer that is selfish and against the will of God is the same as ending a prayer in the name of Kevin or Jim. Powerful prayer is prayer that lines up with God and His Word. That is a prayer that Jesus's name belongs in.

You are from God, little children, and you have conquered them, because the one who is in you is greater than the one who is in the world. (1 John 4:4 CSB)

John penned this line in the midst of encouraging his readers to test the spirits to determine if they are from God or not. He gives the qualification that every spirit that is truly from God will confess that Jesus is the Christ. Any spirit, teacher, evangelist, pastor, worship leader, or prophet who does not confess Jesus as Lord is not from

God but is consumed by the spirit of the Antichrist. That sounds very intimidating and scary, but then John reminds us that we have already conquered them because we belong to God. God is greater than any evil spirit. He is greater than Satan. He is greater than any evil authority in play on this earth. We can be confident in the power and might of our conquering King, and we can partner with Him in His victory.

CHAPTER 3

Money Is the Root of Evil

Discussing money can be very divisive, especially when discussing it within the church or Christian circles. Our phrase for this chapter seems to slip out in conversations relating to a person who made or acquired a large sum of money or is in a career that steadily brings in a hefty salary. I've also heard it quoted with a "told you so" attitude after seeing someone make unwise decisions with money that eventually ruined them financially. Jealousy and gossip typically fuel the fire for this phrase.

People feel good about saying it because they believe it comes from the Bible when it doesn't. This is a misquote of a verse that *is* found in the Bible; however, an important word is left out as well as the entire second part of the verse. The verse in question is 1 Timothy 6:10, which says, "For the love of money is a root of all kinds of evil, and by craving it, some have wandered away from the faith and pierced themselves with many griefs." Paul is addressing the *love of money*, not money itself.

When breaking down a single verse, not only is it important to read the verse in its entirety but also to read the collection of verses around it. So much of our misconceptions about scripture come from taking a single verse at face value or hearing a misquote of a single verse without studying the context in which it was spoken and what was happening in the lives of the speaker and the intended audience.

In the previous verses in chapter 6, Paul is relaying to Timothy the importance of teaching true doctrine and what stems from allowing a false doctrine to be preached and spread. In verse 5, he focuses the attention on people who have joined the faith because they wrongfully believed that seeking God would lead them to financial gain. Greed, rather than desire for God, was fueling their passion for godliness. We see examples of this today with the many churches thriving on teaching a "prosperity gospel."

These churches and pastors proclaim wealth, health, and blessings, without rightfully addressing sin, all while skirting around the teachings of Jesus that assure us that we will face suffering in this world. This teaching results in congregations full of people declaring faith in Jesus simply for the benefits promised. It creates a "vending machine gospel" where we start to view following Jesus as a transaction to receive blessings in return. Another example would be immersing oneself in a church body because of the business or networking connections that are available within.

We can see real-life proof of the second part of 1 Timothy 6:10 by looking at the life of Judas Iscariot. Judas chose to follow Jesus as a disciple during Jesus's time of ministry in the flesh. We learn in John chapter 12 that Judas was the treasurer of the group of disciples and held charge of the money bag. John 12:6 also tells us that Judas was a thief and stole from what was put into the money bag. His greed later led him to betray Jesus into the hands of the chief priest for thirty pieces of silver. His betrayal was what set Jesus's crucifixion into motion.

Knowing that Judas chose to follow Jesus, we can assume that at one time, he had faith in Jesus. His love and desire for money caused him to walk away from Jesus. Greed led him to steal and ultimately led him to betray the One he once followed. Judas learned very quickly that wealth was not what satisfied him. After Jesus was condemned, Judas felt such great remorse that he rid himself of the money he earned by handing Jesus over. He was so tormented by what he had done that he took his own life. What Judas thought would be an easy gain to satisfy his craving for riches brought him to absolute destruction.

Jesus also addresses this topic in Luke 16 as he tells "The Parable of the Dishonest Manager." He speaks a great deal on faithfulness and honesty with wealth, and then in verse 14, the Bible tells us that there were Pharisees listening to Him speak. It is specified that these Pharisees were lovers of money, and because of that love, they scoffed at Jesus. Not only can the love of money cause people to fall away from the faith, but it can also hinder people from genuinely hearing and receiving the truth of Jesus.

Paul teaches in 1 Timothy chapter 6 that learning to be content in what you have *is* great gain and that the ones who desire wealth will fall into temptation, which will lead to destruction. Then we find the verse about the love of money being the root of many evils. Rather than addressing wealth, like so many believe, Paul is truly addressing an issue of devotion. Loving what you receive from God more than you love God Himself is a form of idolatry. Idolatry isn't just an Old Testament problem involving golden calves and sacrifices. Idolatry happens when we place anything on the throne of our hearts other than God. Idols can look like many things including but not limited to social media, sports teams, a marriage, a child, or yes, even money.

When God gave His list of laws to Moses with which he was to govern God's people in Exodus 20:1–17, the very first commandment was "Do not have other gods besides me." God addresses devotion before any other subject, then immediately follows it up with the second commandment, which instructs them not to make an idol in the shape of anything to worship. In verse 5, God says that He is a jealous God. God is not just worthy of our utmost devotion, but He also requires it.

Jesus addressed this while He was on earth several times, but specifically in Matthew 6:24. He says, "No one can serve two masters, since either he will hate one and love the other, or he will be devoted to one and despise the other. You cannot serve both God and money." Again, it is an issue of devotion. There is no straddling the fence in following Jesus. To serve God means to serve Him fully and to serve Him only.

Jesus is explaining "The Parable of the Sower" to His disciples in Mark 4:1–20. He teaches that the seed sown is the Word of God. The Word can grow and produce fruit when planted in the fertile ground of a heart devoted to Him, but if the seed is planted in thorns, it will be choked out and never produce fruit. The thorns He spoke of are worries of this age, the seduction or deceitfulness of wealth, and the desire for other material things. Not only does desiring other things above God lead us into idolatry, but it also limits the fruit we are able to produce from studying His Word.

Looking back at 1 Timothy 6, starting in verse 17, Paul gives these instructions to the rich:

> Instruct those who are rich in the present age not to be arrogant or to set their hope on the uncertainty of wealth, but on God, who richly provides us with things to enjoy. Instruct them to do what is good, to be rich in good works, to be generous and willing to share, storing up treasure for themselves as a good foundation for the coming age, so that they may take hold of what is truly life.

Paul never instructed the rich to rid themselves of all their wealth and material belongings. Paul also never demonized the wealthy. God isn't offended by rich people. He is offended by sinful attitudes within the heart like greed, hatred, pride, and lust. 1 Samuel 16:7 tells us that humans look at the outward appearance, but the Lord sees the heart. Paul does encourage the wealthy to be generous with their belongings because generosity is a characteristic of God and so should be a characteristic of the people who follow Him, whether rich or poor.

Some of you reading are thinking of a specific account in which Jesus instructs a wealthy man to sell all his belongings to follow Him. This event is one that is brought up often when discussing material possessions for Christians, so it is imperative that we dissect it as well. Luke 18:18–30 gives us the full story. A wealthy young ruler comes to Jesus and asks Him how he can receive eternal life. Jesus reminds this ruler of the commandments, and the man assures Jesus that he has kept them all since he was a child. Then Jesus does, in fact, tell the man in verse 22 to sell everything he has, give to the poor, and then follow Him.

We already know from the verse in 1 Samuel that God looks at the heart and motives of a person rather than their outward or fleshly appearance, so we know Jesus, Son of God and part of God, had to be addressing the problem areas within this man rather than problems He had with the man's wealth. How do we know this specifically in this account? Jesus lists adultery, murder, theft, lying, and honoring of parents in this conversation, all of which are included in the commandments. The Ten Commandments never required the people to sell all their possessions and never called it a sin to have wealth, but do you remember what the first commandment does address? Idolatry and devotion.

The one thing this rich young ruler lacked was devotion to God above anything else. His material wealth was an idol. Jesus knew for this man to truly give himself over to a life of following God, he would have to take his wealth off the throne of his heart. Jesus is so personal with us. He knows exactly where you struggle and what you hold dear, just like He knew every part of this man's heart. Jesus was speaking to him in a way that specifically applied to his current situation.

Another interesting thing to note here is that the man came to Jesus desiring eternal life rather than a Savior. His view of Jesus was as a ticket to heaven. My heart breaks thinking of all the people alive right now who see Him in the same way. Jesus never came to be our ticket to eternity. A relationship with Him absolutely secures your eternity with Him, but if we value eternal life over Jesus, our view is skewed. The beauty of eternity is being with our King and Savior with no separation. Jesus came to save us from our sin and the death it brings, but that is the beginning of a life with Him, not the end. He came to be our Savior first and then our Lord.

The young ruler eventually left this encounter with Jesus grieved because of his many possessions. In the moment he walked away, he chose his wealth over the Savior. His heart was too taken by the things he owned to allow a new King to take the throne. Following Jesus will cost something, but the cost is not necessarily money or possessions for every person like it was for this young man. The cost of following Jesus is whatever person, item, or ideal you place above Jesus, and only you can decide if Jesus is worth giving up your devotion to it or not.

Jesus then uses this example to teach about the power of God in verses 24–30. Jesus recognized that the young ruler was grieved and says that it is easier for a camel to go through the eye of a needle than for a rich person to enter heaven. The people listening I'm sure felt hopeless at this revelation and asked, "Then, who can be saved?" Jesus's response puts everything into perspective. In verse 27, He replies, "What is impossible with man is possible with God." Our flesh is not even fully capable of devotion to God without the help of God. What a genuine comfort to know that God fully understands that fact and offers His strength and help as we submit to Him.

Also found in Luke is Jesus's meeting with Zacchaeus found in chapter 19. You may remember him from the children's song as the "wee little man" who climbed a tree to get a glimpse of Jesus. Zacchaeus had a bad reputation among the Jews because of his profession as a tax collector. Tax collectors were employed by Rome to collect the taxes they imposed on the Jewish people. This was enough to garner a negative reaction from the people, but tax collectors were also known for taking more than what was asked to line their own pockets. Tax collectors became very rich because of this deception.

Zacchaeus was not just a tax collector. The Bible tells us that he was a chief tax collector, and he, as was the norm, was rich. He wanted to see Jesus as He passed through Jericho, but a crowd had gathered limiting what Zacchaeus could see because of his short stature. He really did climb a tree just to see Jesus. I can't imagine his surprise when Jesus looks up to the tree and says, "Zacchaeus, hurry and come down because today it is necessary for me to stay at your house."

As Zacchaeus and Jesus set out together, the people were complaining that Jesus was associating with a sinner. Zacchaeus says to

Jesus in verse 8, "Look, I'll give half of my possessions to the poor, Lord. And if I have extorted anything from anyone, I'll pay it back four times as much." Jesus looked at the heart of Zacchaeus and saw true repentance behind his words. We know this because in verse 9, Jesus says to him, "Today salvation has come to this house." Meeting Jesus led Zacchaeus to an accurate view of himself and his ill-gotten gains compared to the Savior. Zacchaeus understood that the real treasure was this Savior who had called him down from the tree, and his wealth held no appeal in comparison.

In Matthew 6:21, Jesus teaches that where your treasure lies shows where your heart lies. If your desire is only for wealth or material possessions, your heart will be consumed with wealth and material possessions. If you put every ounce of your time and energy into a career, that career holds your devotion and your heart. If you have questions about where your devotion lies, evaluate what you deem as a priority. What holds the majority of our attention usually holds the majority of our devotion as well. Jesus reminds us in Matthew 22:37 that the greatest commandment is to love the Lord with all your heart, soul, and mind.

In Matthew 6:25–34, Jesus speaks about possessions again but from a slightly different viewpoint. Here He addresses the worry and anxiety that comes with concern for food, clothing, and drink. He describes how God cares for the birds and clothes the wildflowers in beauty as proof that He will provide for and take care of His children. He knows what we truly need. In verse 33, He says, "But seek first the kingdom of God and His righteousness, and all these things will be provided for you."

Again, order matters in the kingdom of God. Seek God and His righteousness *first*. Seek God above all else. Desire God above all else. Devote yourself to Jesus above all else, and He will take care of what is needed to sustain you. Proverbs 3:5–6 says it like this, "Trust in the Lord with all your heart, and do not rely on your own understanding; in all your ways know him, and he will make your paths straight."

In Mark 12:41–44, we find a story of a poor widow. Her name is never mentioned, and there are only four verses written about her, but her devotion to God moves the heart of Jesus. Jesus sat and watched as person after person came to place their offerings into the treasury at the temple. He saw very wealthy people deposit fittingly large amounts. Then this widowed woman comes and places two small coins into the treasury. The Bible tells us that her two coins had very little worth. This humble offering led Jesus to gather His disciples and say, "Truly I tell you, this poor widow has put more into the treasury than all the others. For they all gave out of their surplus, but she out of her poverty has put in everything she had—all she had to live on."

In the culture of that time, it was incredibly difficult for a woman to survive on her own if she had no husband or grown sons to care for her. The poverty and uncertainty that this woman was living in didn't keep her from offering what she had to God. She was so devoted to the Lord that she gave her all. The rich young ruler proved his devotion to his wealth by walking away from Jesus. This woman proved her devotion to God by not holding back even the last bit she had to live on. God isn't looking for lavish, expensive offerings; He just wants your heart. Jesus saw the richness of her devotion rather than the meager monetary amount of her offering.

The Bible does speak about how we should handle our money as well. In Hebrews 13:5, we are instructed to be content in what we have. Proverbs 21:20 tells us that a wise person saves for the future. Responsibility with our money is important, and our faithfulness, even in worldly wealth, tells of our overall faithfulness. In Luke chapter 16, in Jesus's "Parable of the Dishonest Manager," He says in verses 10–11, "Whoever is faithful in very little is also faithful in much, and whoever is unrighteous in very little is unrighteous in much. So if you have not been faithful worldly wealth, who will trust you in what is genuine?"

In Romans 13:7, it is clearly stated that followers of Jesus should also be responsible in their debts and pay what they owe. In all the references to money and possessions, you will see that the advice to be generous is found often. 1 John 3:17 says, "If anyone has this world's goods and sees a fellow believer in need but withholds compassion from him—how does God's love reside in him?" We are to care for those in need and provide for orphans and widows. We are blessed to bless others.

God also expects us to be faithful in our tithes. Tithing goes all the way back to the Old Testament book of Leviticus. In chapter 27, the people were instructed to bring a tenth of the land's produce to the temple to be set aside for the Lord. In Malachi chapter 3, the Lord speaks of neglecting to tithe as the same as robbing God. His charge to tithe comes with the promise to throw open the floodgates of heaven and pour out blessings on those who are found faithful. This doesn't always mean a material blessing, but I have seen this proven true in my own life with God faithfully providing for me when I felt there was no way ends would meet. God honors obedience and faithfulness from His children.

> Don't store up for yourselves treasures on earth, where moth and rust destroy and where thieves break in and steal. But store up for yourselves treasures in heaven, where neither moth nor rust destroys, and where thieves don't break in and steal. (Matthew 6:19–20 CSB)

So instead of taking inventory of your belongings, take an inventory of your heart. Where is your treasure? Where is your devotion? Are you holding onto and craving wealth, or faithfully serving God with what you have, however little or much that is? God is much less concerned with the amount in your bank account than He is with your love and desire for Him. As Ecclesiastes 5:10 reminds us, "The one who loves silver is never satisfied with silver, and whoever loves wealth is never satisfied with income." Things of earth will never truly satisfy, but a life lived in surrender to the Lord will. Psalm 107:9 says, "For he has satisfied the thirsty and filled the hungry with good things."

The writer of Hebrews again warns against the love of money in chapter 13 verse 5, "Keep your life free from the love of money. Be satisfied with what you have, for he himself has said, 'I will never leave you or abandon you.'" If everything you owned was stripped away in an instant, much like Job, you would still have the richest inheritance. No possessions can compare to the richness that is friendship with God through the salvation of Jesus. His faithfulness is unmatched. His love is deep and devoted for His children. His counsel is invaluable. His salvation is the truest gift, and He has promised He will never leave or abandon the ones who know Him. Anything else we could ever earn or gather in this life is temporary, while communion with Him is eternal.

CHAPTER 4

FOLLOW YOUR HEART

Other variations of this quote include "listen to your heart," "trust your gut," and "trust yourself." The first thing we need to straighten out is what is actually being referred to when we use the word *heart* in this context. Phrases like these are not referring to the physical organ located in the thorax of the body that is responsible for pumping blood to the rest of the vital organs. I think it's well-known that the heart has no ability to think for itself and is at the mercy of the impulses sent from the brain to do the job required of it. When speaking of the heart in a theological or spiritual sense, it represents the mind, will, desires, and emotions.

So from that, we can better understand that our highlighted quote for this chapter is instructing you to follow your emotions, desires, or thoughts on a certain subject. Most often, this phrase is used when facing a tough decision. Think along the lines of relationship decisions, career changes, defining boundaries in a situation, or choosing to pursue something that will bring big changes. The Bible has a lot to say regarding the subject of the human heart in this context.

When looking at the subject of the heart, we need to understand that the heart of humans is what God sees and weighs rather than the outward appearance. We mentioned this in the previous chapter with the verse reference being 1 Samuel 16:7. Psalm 139 gives us a deeper view of what it means for the Lord to look at the heart.

> Lord, you have searched me and known me. You know when I sit down and when I stand up; you understand my thoughts from far away. You observe my travels and my rest; you are aware of all my ways. Before a word is on my tongue, you know all about it, Lord. You have encircled me; you have placed your hand on me. (Psalm 139:1–5 CSB)

God sees every physical move we make, but He also knows each motive behind those movements. He understands our dislikes and what sparks our interests. He thoroughly understands each thought that passes through our minds. He never has to guess the emotion or reasoning behind a statement because He knows it before a word is even spoken. Humans very often take things out of context or read sentiments into conversations that were never there to begin with. God will never be guilty of this because He knows the intent of our thoughts as they are forming before they even exit our mouths as words.

As Solomon is dedicating the newly built temple to the Lord in 2 Chronicles chapter 6, he prays a beautiful prayer on behalf of himself and Israel who will be worshipping the Lord at this temple. In verse 30, he prays, "May you hear from heaven, your dwelling place, and may you forgive and give to everyone according to all their ways, since you know each heart, for you alone know the human heart." God's understanding of our hearts is complete in our communications with others, but it is a deep comfort to know that He understands the heart behind each prayer we bring to Him as well.

A New Testament example of the way the Lord sees the heart can be found in Mark 2:1–12. Jesus was back in Capernaum with his disciples and, as he was teaching, had drawn an incredibly large crowd. The Bible tells us there was no more room in the house He was teaching from. A group of people climbed to the roof of this house, dug through it, and lowered their paralytic friend down on a stretcher through the hole they created in the ceiling. The group was desperate to get their friend to Jesus because they had faith that He was able to heal.

Jesus tells this paralytic man in verse 5 that his sins are forgiven. It was unheard of for a common person to pronounce the forgiveness of sins. Up until this point, sin required an atoning sacrifice offered to God at the temple by a priest on behalf of the person who had sinned to be forgiven. There were scribes, experts of the Jewish law, sitting in attendance, and we learn that Jesus perceived in His spirit that these scribes were questioning Jesus and accusing Him of blaspheming in their hearts. The account never says that the scribes voiced these opinions out loud, only that they thought these things within themselves. Jesus is not separate from God, so He looked inwardly at the hearts, or thoughts, of these men in the same way God looks at the heart.

Knowing that God sees our true thoughts and emotions more thoroughly than we can see them ourselves, the following verse should settle heavily in your mind. Jeremiah 17:9–10 says, "The heart is more deceitful than anything else, and incurable—who can understand it? I, the Lord, examine the mind, I test the heart to give to each according to his way, according to what his actions deserve." In Genesis 6:5, before God sent the great flood, He says that He was grieved that He ever created man because every inclination of their minds was nothing but evil all the time. God sees the clearest picture of our hearts, and what He finds is that our hearts are deceitful and wicked.

Emotions can absolutely be indicators in life, but they should never be allowed to become the final authority in your decisions. Why? Because our emotions are influenced by the flesh, and they lie. Think of how easily your mood can be affected by external or internal conditions. A chaotic commute to work can set a negative tone to the entire day. A few nights of missed sleep can drastically affect not only your health but your clarity of mind as well.

Hunger can drive a person to anger and rash speech. How many times have you heard someone say they can't be trusted in the grocery store on an empty stomach? If our grocery purchases can so easily be affected by the condition of our body, isn't it safe to say that our physical condition and circumstances can affect our emotions and our ability to decipher those emotions as well? Proverbs 29:11 says in the English Standard Version, "A fool gives full vent to his spirit, but a wise man quietly holds it back." Allowing our emotions to take control of our words and actions with no tempering or filtering sets us up for very foolish decision-making.

If you have ever experienced anxiety or depression, you know very well how fickle emotions can be. While struggling through a time of depression, you see people and situations in a much different light than you would when the depression is under control. Anxiety can magnify feelings and fears drastically as well. Proverbs 12:25 confirms this, "Anxiety in a person's heart weighs it down, but a good word cheers it up."

Mark 7:20–22 tells us this, "What comes out of a person is what defiles him. For from within, out of people's hearts come evil thoughts, sexual immoralities, thefts, murders, adulteries, greed, evil actions, deceit, self-indulgence, envy, slander, pride, and foolishness." In the account of the "Sermon on the Mount" found in Matthew chapter 5, Jesus says that murder and adultery begin in the heart. He clarifies that simply looking at another person with lust in your heart is already adultery because the motive behind the thought is impure. Acting upon those thoughts is a sin as well, but that sin was birthed first in the heart.

Humans don't require education on sinning to become adept at sinning. Sin is innate for humanity. Small children are the perfect example of this. Lying comes naturally when they begin to realize there is a potential for scolding because of a decision they made. Experiencing anger can provoke a toddler into hitting or kicking even when that behavior has never been modeled before them. The heart is the birthplace of sin in every human being.

Even David, who would be in the lineage of Jesus and was called a man who was after God's heart, understood the depravity of his own human heart. Psalm 51 was written by David after one of his greatest moral failures. He was king in Israel and saw a beautiful woman, Bathsheba, bathing. His heart desired her, and then from that desire came sinful actions. David, taken by and driven by lust, called for this married woman to be brought to him. Lust moved on to impure intentions, these intentions were acted upon, and she became pregnant. David then went to extreme lengths, ultimately having Bathsheba's husband killed in battle to cover up their sin. David's sin began in his heart and then spilled over into his actions. You can read the full story in 2 Samuel chapters 11 and 12.

In Psalm 51, David is repenting of this sin against God and asking to be restored. In verse 10, he asks God to create a clean heart within him. He saw the wicked parts of himself, and instead of asking God to simply clean his heart, he asked God to create within him an entirely new clean one. Rather than desiring a brand-new organ, we know David was asking God to give him new desires and motives. David knew that the heart of man is inherently wicked and will continue to be so without the help of God.

In Psalm 14, another psalm of David, he says in verse 3 that no one is good and that all have become corrupt. Rest assured, a sinful heart is not a problem unique to a single person or only a select few people. You aren't broken or a lost cause if you struggle with sinful desires, no matter how much Satan would like you to believe that you are. Remember that Adam and Eve faced the temptation and consequences of sin even while living in perfect conditions. Sin is a human issue that we all must deal with on this side of eternity.

After looking at examples of what the Bible says about the heart, I hope you agree that instructing someone to follow that heart is some of the worst possible advice we could ever give, especially as disciples of Jesus. Now what? We know the heart is deceitful and not to be trusted. If we can't trust our own hearts, how are we supposed to make it through these decisions and choices that life is constantly throwing toward us?

Romans 12:2 gives us these instructions: "Do not be conformed to this age, but be transformed by the renewing of your mind, so that you may discern what is the good, pleasing, and perfect will of God." Our minds, wills, and emotions must be transformed and renewed. Don't be discouraged, believing that this is something you must accomplish on your own. It is not possible on your own, but only through the power of the Holy Spirit and the transforming power of the Word of God. Second Corinthians 5:17 encourages us with the news that anyone who is in Christ is a new creation!

> For while we were still helpless, at the right time, Christ died for the ungodly. For rarely will someone die for a just person—though for a good person perhaps someone might even dare to die. But God proves his own love for us that while we were still sinners, Christ died for us. How much more then, since we have now been declared righteous by his blood, will we be saved through him from wrath. For if, while we were enemies, we were reconciled to God through the death of his Son, then how much more, having been reconciled, will we be saved by his life. And not only that, but we also rejoice in God through our Lord Jesus Christ, through whom we have now received this reconciliation. (Romans 5:6–11 CSB)

God is not surprised by your sinful heart. Jesus came because we could never become righteous without Him. His blood was shed to be the atonement for your sin. While you were still a sinner, Jesus came. By confessing your sin, receiving the forgiveness of God through Jesus, and allowing Jesus to become the Lord of your life, you become a new creation. You become an heir with Jesus, a son or daughter of the God of the universe. This is where the transformation begins.

We have the assurance in Philippians 2:13 that, as children of God, God is working in us so that we can work according to His good plans. He works in us through the indwelling Holy Spirit. We must live in the flesh until eternity, but because of the good gift of the Holy Spirit, we no longer must be enslaved to the flesh. While the fruit of the flesh is evil of many kinds and ultimately death, the fruit of the Spirit working inside you is much more beautiful.

> I say then, walk by the Spirit and you will certainly not carry out the desires of the flesh. For the flesh desires what is against the Spirit, and the Spirit desires what is against the flesh; these are opposed to each other, so that you don't do what you want. But if you are led by the Spirit, you are not under the law. Now the works of the flesh are obvious: sexual immorality, moral impurity, promiscuity, idolatry, sorcery, hatreds, strife, jealousy, outbursts of anger, selfish ambitions, dissensions, factions, envy, drunkenness, carousing, and anything similar. I am warning you about these things—as I warned you before—that those who practice such things will not inherit the kingdom of God. But the fruit of the Spirit is love, joy, peace, patience, kindness, goodness, faithfulness, gentleness, and self-control. (Galatians 5:16–23 CSB)

These beautiful attributes of the Spirit can only be added to your character by being yielded to and obedient to the Holy Spirit working inside you. You can only truly embody these characteristics when you are being led by the Spirit. We discussed earlier how the Holy Spirit brings us power against the enemy, but here we learn that the Spirit also gives us power to deny our own flesh and live a life surrendered to God.

John chapter 1 tells us that the Word was with God in the beginning, and the Word was God. Jesus came as the Word made flesh to dwell on earth among humanity. We know that God is not separate from Jesus or from the Holy Spirit. Here we learn that God is not separate from His Word either. This means that the Holy Spirit is not separate from the Word. Jesus tells the disciples in John 14:26 that the Holy Spirit will remind them of the words He spoke to them. The Words Jesus spoke live in the perfectly bound pages of our Bible. The Holy Spirit can't remind us of something we've never taken the initiative to study, so living in step with the Holy Spirit will also require devotion to the Word of God.

The Holy Spirit is also known as the Teacher, and it's His job to teach you about the Word you study as He empowers you to live out what the Word calls for. Jesus tells the woman at the well in John chapter 4 that God is Spirit and that those who worship Him must worship in Spirit and in truth. Both are necessary. You cannot live out truths that you haven't taken the time to learn. Becoming a student of the Word of God will give you the ability to compare your thoughts, emotions, and desires to the truth of God's Word. Then the Holy Spirit will empower you to align your heart and actions to those truths.

> For the word of God is living and effective and sharper than any double-edged sword, penetrating as far as the separation of soul and spirit, joints and marrow. It is able to judge the thoughts and intentions of the heart. (Hebrews 4:12 CSB)

Because God's Word is a part of God, the truths held within our Bible are much more than old words printed in new ink. The stories and proverbs held inside are not just history lessons. The words contained in the pages of our Bibles are alive, eternal, and powerful. God's standards are the only standards worthy to compare our human emotions and feelings to. Because this Word is a part of God, the Word can be used to judge our own thoughts and intentions.

In Philippians chapter 2, Paul reminds us in verse 15 that we are to be blameless and pure children of God in the middle of a crooked generation by holding firm to God's Word. In fact, he says that we can only stand out among this evil generation by holding on to the Word. The only way we begin to look less like flesh and more like Jesus is by loving God's Word and living out what it says while being empowered by the Holy Spirit.

We cannot trust our own fleshly hearts, desires, or emotions, but we *can* trust God. We can trust the Spirit He sent to dwell within us and guide us. We can trust the Son who came to provide and sacrifice for our salvation and is now interceding on our behalf. We can trust the Word of God that is part of God and holds all the truth we need to choose the ways of God over our fleshly instincts.

Within the poetic words of the Psalms, we can see a glimpse of human writers experiencing human emotion in the same way we do even in the psalms written by David. He was a man after God's own heart, but he was still a man. He, and the other psalmists, were familiar with pain, fear, anxiety, depression, heartbreak, anger, uncertainty, and joy. One thing I love about the Psalms is that even amid extreme circumstances and emotions, the writers often take the time to remind their own souls to fall in line with the will of God and worship. One example of that is found in Psalm 42. Multiple times throughout chapter 42 and even into chapter 43 it says, "Why, my soul, are you so dejected? Why are you in such turmoil? Put your hope in God, for I will still praise him, my Savior and my God."

Acknowledge your emotion as the psalmist did. Even Jesus wept when feeling pain and was moved by compassion when He encountered the pain of others. As mentioned earlier, emotions can absolutely be indicators, given that we weigh what we feel against the truth of God's Word. This psalmist recognizes that he is dismayed and experiencing inner turmoil yet reminds himself that his hope is in God and chooses to praise rather than continue in despair. It is a perfect picture of surrendering human will to the will of God. Your emotions may proclaim things that go against the Word of God, but by becoming a student of God and living in step with the Spirit, you will begin to recognize it.

Store up His Word in your heart and evaluate every thought, emotion, and desire you have against what His Word says. Ask God to reveal any places in your heart that do not line up with His heart and then rely on His strength to help you knowingly choose the ways of God rather than the ways of your flesh. I mentioned Psalm 139 earlier in this chapter. It's another beautiful psalm written by David, and later in verses 23 and 24, David asks the Lord to search his heart and see if there is any offensive way within him. Then he asks God to lead him in the way that is everlasting. The ways of God are everlasting. The ways of the flesh have an unpleasant end. Repentance is the first step in seeing your desires become matched to God's desires.

When you find yourself being asked for advice by a friend or family member, rather than recommending they follow the deceit of their hearts, open your Bible. Pray before you offer any advice. Ask God to reveal to you the words He would have you say and the encouragement that lines up with the truth of His word. Sure, it's easy to offer our own thoughts on a situation, but it is so much more powerful to offer the life-giving truth of God's Word.

CHAPTER 5

I Love Jesus, but I Cuss a Little

I want to apologize in advance for this chapter because I know this one will step on some toes. Like I said in the introduction, the Word of God will be offensive to the areas in our hearts and lives that pale in comparison to its truth. "I love Jesus, but I cuss a little" is a very popular statement. I've seen it printed across T-shirts, shared humorously on social media, and heard it joked about in conversations. Typically, the motive behind this one is an attempt to downplay shortcomings or areas you know you should change but are reluctant to.

This phrase could be used in a variety of ways with a variety of different sins in the place of cursing. The problems with it remain the same no matter what vice we insert. However, let's first take it at face value and look deeper at what the Bible says about our words, cursing, and vulgar language specifically and then break down the problems with the phrase overall.

The biggest argument I hear regarding cursing, and negative speech in general is that words are only words. People argue that humans have given a negative connotation to certain words and made them vulgar or offensive, so in their minds, speech is not a faith issue. Another often-used argument is that the Bible doesn't list any specific words as off-limits. While this is true and you won't find a list of curse words to avoid in the index of your Bible, God does have a lot to say about the impact of our words.

> And consider ships: Though very large and driven by fierce winds, they are guided by a very small rudder wherever the will of the pilot directs. So too, though the tongue is a small part of the body, it boasts great things. Consider how a small fire sets ablaze a large forest. And the tongue is a fire. The tongue, a world of unrighteousness, is placed among our members. It stains the whole body, sets the course of life on fire, and is itself set on fire by hell. (James 3:4–6 CSB)

Just as we discovered the deceitfulness and wickedness of the heart in the previous chapter, these verses give us good insight into the true nature of words that flow from the flesh. It is strong language to say that the tongue is a world of unrighteousness. Stronger still to say that it is set on fire by hell itself. Words are much more than expressions with little importance or impact.

Proverbs 18:21 says, "Death and life are in the power of the tongue, and those who love it will eat its fruit." If our words can either hold death or life, which are two very serious subjects, I think it's safe to say that what we speak matters and carries weight in the world around us. Earlier in Proverbs 15:4, a gentle tongue is described as a tree of life, while perverseness or a devious tongue is said to break the spirit. Proverbs 16:24 says, "Pleasant words are a honeycomb: sweet to the taste and health to the body." Even the spirit and physical body can be affected by words. Colossians 4:6 encourages us to let our speech always be gracious.

Paul describes the followers of Jesus who speak and preach the gospel as the fragrance of Christ in 2 Corinthians 2:15. He goes on to say that to the hearers who choose to believe in Christ, the message is the aroma of life. Our words can carry death, or they can carry life, and it's up to us to choose which we take part in. Not only that, but when we choose our words in ways that honor God, we get the privilege of being called the very fragrance of Jesus.

Jesus teaches in Matthew 12:33–37 that our words flow directly from the heart, meaning that what we store up in our hearts will eventually come out of our mouths. He also warns that our words can either acquit or condemn us. Our words not only bring life or death to the hearer, but they also give a glimpse into our own spiritual health. James touches on this in verse 2 of chapter 3 as well. Our words reveal our spiritual maturity.

Ephesians 4:29 says: "No foul language should come from your mouth, but only what is good for building up someone in need, so that it gives grace to those who hear." In the English Standard Version, the term *corrupting talk* is used in place of *foul language*. The section this verse comes from in Ephesians chapter 4 is giving instructions on how to live fully the new life of following Jesus rather than living and looking like the culture of the world that doesn't know Him. Knowing that most of the world around us could name several specific words as curse words, foul language, or simply offensive in nature, how can we justify their use as appropriate for someone who has claimed new life through salvation from Jesus?

The last part of verse 29 gives us the key to how we should evaluate every word that comes from our mouths. Are the words I'm saying building up and giving grace to the hearer? If not, the Bible is clear that they should never exit our mouths. In this world driven by technology, that means they should never be sent in a text message from our phones or shared on social media either. The speech we use can either portray Christ, or it can portray the flesh. Putting this kind of filter over our words requires a much deeper look at what we say than simply eliminating cursing.

Gossip is corrupting talk. Speaking vulgarly or making inappropriate jokes is corrupting talk. Lying is corrupting talk. Slander, hateful speech, disrespectful comments, and harsh outbursts fueled by anger are all corrupting talk. Husbands and wives, speaking disrespectfully about your respective spouse is corrupting talk. Grumbling and complaining are corrupting talk as well.

We are called to a much higher standard as bearers of the name of Jesus. James 1:26 puts it boldly in this way, "If anyone thinks he is religious without controlling his tongue, his religion is useless and he deceives himself." If I cannot control what comes from my mouth, any semblance of religion I possess is useless. If I cannot control my words, no one will want any part of the Jesus I claim. The power of life and death is in the tongue.

Your words have the power to kill your testimony. Your words have the power to destroy your witness. They may only be words to you, but you have people around you who don't believe in or haven't met Jesus. Those people are watching you closely to see if the things you claim to portray are true or not. One of the most effective ways to display the love of Christ is through our words. Keep in mind that our actions must back up our words as well. The way we handle situations that anger or hurt us, in word and deed, will speak loudly of the depth of the love of Christ that is within us.

Jumping to the complete opposite side of the scale, did you know that God addresses not only corrupting talk but fake speech that masquerades as holy speech as well?

> These people approach me with their speeches to honor me with lip-service—yet their hearts are far from me, and human rules direct their worship of me. (Isaiah 29:13 CSB)

Jesus references this verse from Isaiah again in Matthew 15 as He is addressing problems with the way the scribes and Pharisees break the commandments of God to hold onto their tradition. Then in Ezekiel 33, God speaks of this same theme to Ezekiel. In verse 31, He says, "So my people come to you in crowds, sit in front of you, and hear your words, but they don't obey them. Their mouths go on passionately, but their hearts pursue dishonest profit." Any time you find repetition in the Bible, pay attention! God places emphasis on things for a reason.

Switching back to the New Testament, in Matthew chapter 6, we see Jesus addressing faults with hypocrites. He warns about showy displays of giving and long-winded public prayers full of empty words. We already know that God sees the heart. No amount of "Christian jargon" can hide a heart full of pride and sinful desires from God. This is a reminder to us not only to guard our mouths but to start by guarding our hearts. Honoring God in your heart by obedience and reverence can't help but spill over into your speech. The mouth speaks from what is stored up in the heart.

There are so many different personalities in the world. Some people are timid and more reluctant to speak, even when they probably should, while others say what they are thinking with no filter or any real thought to their words. I have encountered people who claimed to be blunt but were truthfully only relying on that label to say whatever they wanted without feeling responsible for any pain they caused with their words. Handing over our words to be sifted by the Lord will sometimes require us to speak when we would rather not, but other times, it will require us to shut up when we would really like to add our commentary. Proverbs 25:11 backs this up, saying, "A word spoken at the right time is like gold apples in silver settings." It is beautiful when our words come when they are truly needed.

The Holy Spirit empowers us with the authority of Jesus to do many incredible things, but we are selling Him short if we miss the fact that He also wants to help us control our words. As we discussed previously, self-control is a fruit of the Spirit, meaning the Spirit will help us to gain self-control as we walk in step with the Spirit. Proverbs 21:23 says, "The one who guards his mouth and tongue keeps himself out of trouble."

In Jeremiah chapter 15, God calls Jeremiah to repent and gives him this charge in verse 19, "If you return, I will take you back; you will stand in my presence. And if you speak noble words, rather than worthless ones, you will be my spokesman." While his struggle was not with cursing or gossip, Jeremiah was called to speak things that would not be very popular to the people around him. Jeremiah had many hard truths from God to share with his people who had wandered far from the ways of God. Jeremiah struggled with the messages but was faithful in the end to speak what God instructed him to. God called Jeremiah's attention to the importance of his words, just as He is drawing our attention to that fact as well.

Worthless words are just that: worthless. They have no value on earth or in eternity. In the end, when we stand in the presence of our holy God, the gossip we took part in will look like filth. We will realize the worthlessness of the lies we told and the curse words we allowed to fly carelessly. We will see the hurt we caused other people with our speech when we had the opportunity to use our words to build them up with truth instead. When we see the face of our sweet, beautiful Jesus, we will wish we had used our time on earth to speak noble words that glorified Him every chance we were given. We will realize that He is worth learning to control our tongues and so much more.

> With the tongue we bless our Lord and Father, and with it we curse people who are made in God's likeness. Blessing and cursing come out of the same mouth. My brothers and sisters, these things should not be this way. Does a spring pour out sweet and bitter water from the same opening? Can a fig tree produce olives, my brothers and sisters, or a grapevine produce figs? Neither can a saltwater spring yield fresh water. (James 3:9–12 CSB)

We cannot pour out blessings and praise one minute and then curses the next and expect this state of duplicity to honor or impress God. As much as the words we say matter, the motive behind those words is just as important. God sees the heart, as we have covered in depth in previous chapters. If your speech doesn't match what you proclaim, there is a problem to be addressed. We cannot claim to love God and treat or speak of the people made in His image like garbage. One of the simplest ways to evaluate your love for people is by evaluating your words.

While loving people with our speech will absolutely require restraint in the things we say, it will also require the willingness to speak the truth in necessary times as well. Just as Jeremiah had hard truths to relay, speaking truth will also be required of us. Truly filtered speech will be seasoned with grace and compassion while relaying the truth with no compromise. There is no greater way to love another person than in speech by sharing the truth of Jesus with them.

Language may be something you have no problem with, but if it is, I hope you don't feel condemned by what I've written. There is grace for our shortcomings, no matter how great of a hold they have on us. In Psalm 19:14, David prays, "May the words of my mouth and the meditation of my heart be acceptable to you, Lord, my rock and my Redeemer." Take this scripture and begin to pray it for yourself daily, hourly, or as often as you feel the need. Surrendering your speech to the Lord will allow Him to help you take control of it. Fill your heart and mind with the words of God, and you will begin to see glimpses of the Lord when you open your mouth rather than glimpses of the flesh.

Another benefit in being yielded to God and filled with His Spirit is that the Spirit will not only help you control your tongue, but He will also give you the words to say when needed. In Luke 12, Jesus is speaking to the disciples about the persecution that will come to them because of their devotion to Him. He tells them in verses 11–12 not to worry about what they will say when brought before leaders and rulers to defend themselves because the Holy Spirit will teach them what to say at the very hour they need it. In John 14:26, we even have the promise that the Holy Spirit will bring the words of Jesus to our remembrance in the perfect time.

God won't command us to do something that He can't or won't empower us to do when we are living in obedience to Him. If He is telling you to gain control of your tongue, He is prepared to help you through the process. If you feel the nudge from the Holy Spirit that it's time to eliminate gossip from your life, He will provide the strength to carry it out. If you desire to speak what is precious instead of what is worthless, become a student of the Word of God and ask Him to help you live in the way the Word instructs. God is not a distant King with requirements we can never hope to achieve; He is a close intimate Father who longs to help His children grow in His ways.

Now, let's dig into our featured phrase and the reason I chose to include it. "I love Jesus, but I cuss a little" goes much farther beyond saying you love Jesus, but you aren't perfect. This statement is essentially saying you've declared your love for Jesus, but you still live in sin. There is a huge difference in simply sinning and living in sin. We sin because we are flesh; in fact, we will struggle with sin until we are with Jesus in eternity.

As redeemed followers of Jesus, sin should break our hearts and draw us to repentance. Repentance is not just offering God an apology. Repenting means that you see the error in your way, lay it down before the Lord for forgiveness, and then turn the opposite direction of that sin. Not to say that you will never struggle with that sin again, but continuing in the sin with no changes in your behavior is a good indicator that you apologized yet never followed through with true repentance.

> If we say, "We have fellowship with him," and yet we walk in darkness, we are lying and not practicing the truth. If we walk in the light as he himself is in the light, we have fellowship with one another, and the blood of Jesus his Son cleanses us from all sin. If we say, "We have no sin," we are deceiving ourselves, and the truth is not in us. If we confess our sins, he is faithful and righteous to forgive us our sins and to cleanse us from all unrighteousness. (1 John 1:6–9 CSB)

Living in sin is a consistent choosing of sin daily with no remorse or action to correct or change it. When we receive the Holy Spirit, not only is He here to teach us and comfort us, but He is here to correct us as well. He comes with conviction when we do sin so that we can repent and make the necessary changes to correct the behavior before it becomes a lifestyle. Consistently choosing sin is walking in the darkness when we've been called to walk in the light.

When we say, "I love Jesus, but I (fill in the blank)," we are basically saying that our love for Jesus isn't strong enough to give up our love for a specific sin. Including that tiny little "but" in the phrase is proof that the speaker agrees that the following action is a sin. There would be no reason to address it in contrast to love for Jesus if it were a godly quality. Sin is sin, no matter how large or small. In James 2:10, we learn that stumbling in one part of the law makes us guilty of it all. So saying, "I love Jesus, but I cuss a little" is the same as saying, "I love Jesus, but I murder a little," or "I love Jesus, but I steal things." That sounds absurd to us, but to God sin is equal.

God takes sin very seriously because sin is why Jesus had to die. Sin is what brought the curse of death into the creation that He deemed good. Sin is a small word with big, costly consequences. Sin was extremely costly for Jesus, and it is costly for us as well. In Matthew 5:30, Jesus says that if your hand causes you to sin, it's better to cut it off and face life without a hand than to continue in sin. Sins that we view as small or less harmful are still sins, and all sin leads to death.

Sin has a way of creating calluses in our minds and hearts. A small sin left unchecked begins to seem less offensive to us over time and creates in us a desire for more sin. In Ephesians 4:19, Paul describes people living in sin as people who "gave themselves over to promiscuity for the practice of every kind of impurity with a desire for more and more." When we believe the little sins are safe, it simply paves the way for bigger sins to begin showing up in our everyday lives. Occasional sin that isn't addressed with God becomes a lifestyle.

> My little children, I am writing you these things so that you may not sin. But if anyone does sin, we have an advocate with the Father—Jesus Christ the righteous one. He himself is the atoning sacrifice for our sins, and not only for ours, but also for those of the whole world. This is how we know that we know him: if we keep his commands. The one who says, 'I have come to

> know him,' and yet doesn't keep his commands, is a liar, and the truth is not in him. But whoever keeps his word, truly in him the love of God is made complete. This is how we know we are in him: The one who says he remains in him should walk just as he walked. (1 John 2:1–6 CSB)

We are not expected to live perfectly. God knows that we will struggle with and sometimes give in to sin even after we have chosen to follow Jesus. The problem comes when we begin to accept our sin as an unalterable part of who we are. Sin cannot be something we boast as a character trait. John 8:34 tells us in the English Standard Version that anyone who practices sin is a slave to sin. Practicing something means to perform or carry out this thing habitually or regularly. Continually practicing sin makes sin the lord of your life rather than God. Sin desires slaves, while God desires children.

Slavery is being controlled, while sonship is being taught and nurtured. Discipline and rules are a part of sonship because just as any parent knows, a child cannot be left alone to do whatever they please. However, discipline with pure intentions is required to raise a child into an adult who is capable of surviving and thriving in the society in which they live. If I instruct my daughter to hold on to my hand instead of running alone through a busy parking lot, it isn't to limit her fun or keep her from independence. It is to protect her life. My neglect in teaching her about safety could result in her being struck and killed by a car. God teaches us about the dangers of a lifestyle of sin for the very same reason.

As professing Christians, we are to live a life that is continually sanctified and renewed by God through the power of His Spirit and His Word as we learn in 2 Thessalonians 2:13. Jesus prayed in John 17 before His death that His disciples would be sanctified by the truth, God's Word. Paul said in Romans 15:16 that he ministered to the gentiles for them to be presented to God sanctified by the Holy Spirit. Once again, we see unity in the way the Word of God and Holy Spirit work together for our spiritual benefit.

Sanctification is the process of becoming holy or becoming like Jesus. It is a *process*. You will not be fully sanctified until you cross into eternity with Jesus, but the process should be happening while here on earth. Early in my walk with Jesus, I let many small sins slide thinking they were harmless. As I grow in maturity in Christ, His Word, and in familiarity with the Holy Spirit, I have seen the importance of allowing those things to be pruned from my behavior. None of those modifications can be counted to my credit. It is only by the kindness of God, which leads me to repentance as I walk in His ways.

> As obedient children, do not be conformed to the desires of your former ignorance. But as the one who called you is holy, you also are to be holy in all your conduct; for it is written, "Be holy, for I am holy." (1 Peter 1:14–16 CSB)

God desires holiness from me. He desires holiness from all His children because He is holy. Holiness does not mean perfection with no failures or slip ups; it is a constant devotion to God and pursuit to be like Him in our conduct until the day we are fully sanctified in eternity. Remember He knows you fully and understands that without His help, you have no chance at becoming like Him. He provided us with every support, tool, and strength needed to live holy.

The beautiful part about allowing God to sanctify us is that, as we submit to Him and allow Him to change our desires to His desires, it becomes much less about following rules and more about loving God and loving like Him. Following the ways of God isn't the same as following the rules of your job or school where the responsibility rests solely on your shoulders to carry out. God is so faithful that as we submit to Him and to His discipline, He helps us in every way to live a life that is pleasing to Him. Not only that, but He satisfies and sustains us along the way. His provision is perfect even within His discipline.

Our sin is the reason Jesus came to be our Savior. Sin leads to death, and without the blood of a perfect sacrifice, we could never be brought into communion with God. When we receive the salvation of Jesus, Galatians 5:24 tells us that we have died to sin and have crucified the desire of the flesh. We are dead to sin and, just as Jesus tells us in Luke 9:23, we must take up our cross daily. It is a conscious choice to crucify our sin daily and choose the righteousness of God.

> So of anyone purifies himself from anything dishonorable, he will be a special instrument, set apart, useful to the master, prepared for every good work. Flee from youthful passions, and pursue righteousness, faith, love, and peace, along with those who call on the Lord from a pure heart. (2 Timothy 2:21–22 CSB)

I can think of no greater honor than to be considered a special instrument by God. I can think of no greater calling than to be useful to the Master and prepared for every good work He has planned for me. How could I be content continuing in a sin that I know Jesus died for when He is asking me to crucify that sin and pursue righteousness? God does not expect us to live perfectly, but He does expect us to crucify our flesh daily. Remember, He would never instruct us to do something that He was not planning to empower and strengthen us to do. As we learned in the very first chapter, God's strength is what sustains us, not our own.

In the days before Jesus came and died on the cross, the Jewish people were required to bring an offering for sacrifice to atone for their sin. The priest would offer the sacrifices on the altar before God, and the people would be forgiven. Jesus's sacrifice was the final, necessary sacrifice to atone for the sin of the entire world. No longer do we require the middleman of a human priest to address our sin with God. We now have Jesus as our great high priest and intercessor. Because of Jesus, we can come to God and repent and make our requests known.

In 1 Samuel 15:22, the prophet Samuel tells Saul, "Does the Lord take pleasure in burnt offerings and sacrifices as much as in obeying the Lord? Look: to obey is better than sacrifice, to pay attention is better than the fat of rams." Samuel later goes on to tell Saul that he would be rejected as the king of Israel because he had rejected the Word of the Lord. God desires and deserves our obedience. God values His Word because it is eternally part of Him, and He values when we are obedient to His Word. No amount of public good deeds will bring you into righteousness if you are not obedient in learning and living out the things the Word of God calls for. It starts in the heart.

The better version of "I love Jesus, but I cuss a little" is "I love Jesus so much that I choose not to cuss anymore." Like I mentioned earlier, substitute cussing for whatever area you struggle in. Rather than valuing the sin over the Savior, we have to learn that our Savior is worth giving up the things He asks us to give up. Sin leads to death. There is no way around it. We cannot continue to glorify sin. Jesus is life. His ways are life. The sleeping world will be awakened to the love and life of Jesus by seeing sincere followers of Jesus truly repent and begin to crucify our sin and follow Jesus.

One more side street I want to stroll down briefly for this one is the argument that showing unbelievers that you sin too makes Christians look more inclusive and less judgmental. I completely understand the desire to make people feel like they belong and have importance while in your company, but disobeying God is never the way to accomplish that. The gospel is inclusive enough on its own. The message is open to any and every one.

We are doing a massive disservice to unbelievers by displaying sin more freely than grace and truth. Jesus never took part in sin to bring someone into the fold. He dined with sinners, but never compromised to make an impact. His love and the way He shared the truth was enough. Paul gives the reminder in Romans 6:1 that it makes no sense to continue in sin so that grace may abound. We display the grace and mercy of Christ best by crucifying our sin and being an example of the love of Jesus. There is no better proof of the transforming power of Jesus than seeing a person truly transformed because of a relationship with Jesus.

CHAPTER 6

You Have to Build a Relationship with a Person to Share the Gospel with Them

We, in the modern church, are experts at taking examples from the Bible and creating methods and formulas from them on how to evangelize and reach the lost. This is not wrong at face value; however, we encounter a problem when our methods and formulas begin to say something other than what the Word teaches us. This idea that sharing the gospel with someone requires an established relationship has been circulating heavily recently.

I am in no way trying to take away the value in building relationships with people. Our God is relational. Jesus modeled a life on earth that was very relational. The problem with this method is that it puts emphasis on relationship first and sharing the gospel second when that was never the way Jesus approached reaching people while on earth. We can learn so much from the way Jesus ministered on earth and the way His disciples carried the gospel to the world after Jesus ascended to heaven.

First things first, what does the word *gospel* mean? In Greek, the meaning of the word *gospel* is simply "good news." The gospel is the good news of Jesus. It's the revelation of Jesus Christ as the Messiah who came to earth, died for the sins of the world, was buried and then resurrected, and is coming back for His bride. Sharing the gospel is sharing the fact that because of Jesus, there is hope for humanity.

As we begin to dig into this topic, the first thing we need to understand is that there is a significant difference in evangelizing and discipling. Evangelizing is sharing the gospel. This can be done anywhere, anytime, to anyone. Discipleship is forming a relationship with and guiding another person through following Jesus. Jesus gave us examples of both in His ministry on earth.

Hearing the word *evangelism* is sure to draw some specific images to your mind. It's easy to think of traveling suit-and-tie preachers, pocket-size tracts listing the steps to salvation, and scripts meant to ease you into sharing the gospel effectively. A myriad of books has been written on the subject. You are sure to find classes on evangelism in churches all over the world. If we strip it down to its simplest form, without all the methods and props, evangelism is sharing your faith and hope in Jesus.

All throughout the four Gospels of Matthew, Mark, Luke, and John, we see Jesus teaching large crowds, healing and encouraging people who approached Him on the street, and preaching in the synagogues. These are just a few examples of evangelism. Jesus was sharing the good news of the gospel with anyone who chose to listen. A large portion of these people were strangers to Jesus. Some lived in towns he had never visited prior and most likely never had a private conversation with Him. He had no personal relationship with them as a human. Granted Jesus being the Son of God means that a personal relationship with Him and the Father would be available spiritually, but in the flesh, they were strangers. They had no close relationship with Him in the flesh, yet He still offered the truth to them.

To get an example of discipleship, we must look at the people who followed Jesus closely. Jesus had many people who followed Him, but there were twelve men who were aptly called His disciples. These men walked with Him, learned from Him, shared meals with Him, and studied how to minister directly from Him. They each had intimate relationships with the person of Jesus, so much so that they called Him their rabbi or teacher. From Jesus's example we can gather that you cannot disciple someone without a relationship, but the good news of Jesus can be shared whether there is a close relationship or not.

> But in your hearts regard Christ the Lord as holy, ready at any time to give a defense to anyone who asks you for a reason for the hope that is in you. Yet do this with gentleness and respect, keeping a clear conscience, so that when you are accused, those who disparage your good conduct in Christ will be put to shame. (1 Peter 3:15–16 CSB)

We are called to be prepared to share our hope with *anyone*. If you follow Jesus, hope is personal for you because He is your hope! The gospel of Jesus is our only hope. If you are saved, you were called out of death into the resurrection and the life of Jesus Christ. You were washed in the blood of Jesus your Savior. Your eternity is secure because Jesus was the propitiation for your sin. You can walk boldly and hopefully into uncertain times because of the Spirit of God at work within you and the transforming power of the Word of God. This is good news! Everyone deserves the chance to hear about this good news whether you have known them all your life or met them once, waiting in line for tickets to a movie.

First Peter 3:15 not only tells us that this good news is for anyone but also for any time. Be prepared to share your hope even in the most mundane circumstances. I've seen God open doors for kingdom conversations to happen in the checkout line at Walmart or the waiting area of an automotive shop. When Jesus is the most influential person in your life, sharing Him becomes second nature if you learn to pay attention to the Holy Spirit and what is going on around you.

A friend of mine recently experienced the nudge of the Holy Spirit like this as she waited for her turn to check out in a small store. The shirt she was wearing had a Bible verse written on it, and another waiting customer noticed it, read the scripture, and commented to my friend that they had been experiencing difficult circumstances. My friend didn't push the conversation, but as she was exiting the store, she was certain that God was prompting her to encourage this person. She acted in obedience and was able to speak life into this person's situation and encourage them in the Lord. It was a quick and simple conversation, but the impact made by her obedience is incalculable.

Our Creator sent His only Son into the world to save the world. His message is for every single person. His invitation is open to all. John 3:16 says, "For God loved the world in this way: He gave his one and only Son, so that everyone who believes in him will not perish but have eternal life." How can we not share that news every time the opportunity presents itself? It would be a disservice for me to believe that someone needs to get to know me before I can introduce them to Him.

While we are called to tell everyone about Jesus, we need to keep in mind that there are appropriate ways to do so that honor and glorify God and care for the hearer. The second part of verse 15 in 1 Peter chapter 3 gives us instructions on how we should handle sharing Jesus with others. We must share Jesus with gentleness and respect. Your kind and loving treatment of people is what will usually open the door for someone to listen to the words you speak. We must keep in mind that our lives should show a pattern of gentleness and respect. We cannot live in anger and treat people rudely in our everyday lives and then flip a switch to kindness when we want to share about Jesus.

If you know someone who works in the restaurant industry, chances are you have heard horror stories of people who came into the restaurant where they worked, were demanding and rude, and treated their server as someone beneath them. These same people might leave a card inviting their server to attend their church that said something along the lines of "Jesus loves you!" on the table alongside their tip. Do you think the message of Jesus's love was received well after witnessing the rude actions of a person who claims to love and serve Jesus as a part of the church?

In the time that I have been following Jesus, I have had similar encounters with people outside of a church and then later learned that they were faithful church attenders in the area. Wrongly on my part, I instantly had a negative feeling about their church based on my encounter with one member. Unfortunately, though, that is how much of the world reacts when we, as people who claim Jesus, react sinfully rather than in the way Jesus calls us to.

I'm sure you've all seen negative examples of "street corner ministry." This usually involves handmade signs and a bullhorn while people shout condemning phrases about lifestyles that involve sin or simply ideals they personally disagree with. I have never witnessed this scene and felt drawn to a conversation with these people. In fact, it typically encourages me to walk the opposite direction. If your ministry tactic even scares away people who already truly know Jesus, there is little to no chance it positively impacts a lost person toward Jesus. Your ministry must sincerely display the hope and love of Jesus through your life, words, and actions, or it will not be effective.

Living like Jesus is being a living example of truth and love. If you decide to tell another person about Jesus after they have witnessed you berate a cashier, I can assure you that person will want little to do with the Jesus you proclaim. Your life is your greatest witness. Your actions should proclaim Jesus before you ever open your mouth to speak. Keep in mind what we discovered in the previous chapter. The Holy Spirit will give you the words necessary when you are to speak but also let you know when it's best not to utter a word.

> For you were called to be free, brothers and sisters; only don't use this freedom as an opportunity for the flesh, but serve one another through love. For the whole law is fulfilled in one statement: Love your neighbor as yourself. (Galatians 5:13–14 CSB)

Jesus walked on earth humbly. He served the people He met people whether He was closely associated with them or not. He loved the ones who seemed the hardest to love while still declaring the truth of the Word of God. He has called us to do the same. One of the most impactful things I've ever heard my pastor say is "Love without truth is compromise, and truth without love is condemnation." Jesus shared the truth with no sugarcoating, but He did it in perfect love. If we claim to bear His name, we must live in a way that bears His attributes as well. This is the way to begin evangelizing. The root of sharing the gospel of Jesus must be love. Jesus says in John 13:35 that people will know we are disciples of His if we love one another.

We don't have to overcomplicate sharing our faith. As a teenager who was involved in youth group during high school, I had incredible leaders who did their best to teach us effective and sincere ministry. One story I think of often is a trip our youth group was on together. We stopped at a fast-food restaurant to eat, and as we were leaving, a young man in our group held the door open for a stranger who was exiting the restaurant as well. He smiled and displayed genuine kindness to this stranger, which led the person to thank him and comment that he smiled a lot. The kid in my group responded that he was just happy. Later, our youth pastor lovingly used that situation as an example of an unexpected opportunity to share our faith.

He reminded us that we don't have to prepare a sermon or presentation or make things super-spiritual or theological. In fact, when the stranger commented on my friend's frequent kindness and smile, a simple answer of "I can smile because I have joy from Jesus" would've been enough to intrigue this stranger. A small comment like that could be what opens the door for someone to seek out this Jesus who brings genuine joy to a teenage kid. Jesus is our hope of glory, and the joy that comes from a relationship with Him speaks loudly.

We most likely will only cross paths with some people once or twice in our entire lives. It would be impossible to create a deep, meaningful relationship with every person you meet. However, it's not impossible to be an example of Jesus to every single person you meet, no matter how brief the encounter. A small comment about Jesus from a person displaying the love of Jesus can have a greater impact than we could ever imagine here on earth. The love of Jesus is the difference maker.

There are some people who will ignore every word you say, but genuine love cannot be ignored. In some cases, the more you speak, the less likely someone is to listen. Our culture places such an emphasis on being able to "talk the talk," and social media gives such a broad platform to do so, that I'm afraid people have grown tired of hearing the drone of words with no backing actions to prove them. It's time for the bride of Jesus to abandon empty speech that fits the culture and start loving the world like Jesus even outside the walls of their home churches.

We have to keep in mind that people are unique. You will come in contact with people who have had wonderful examples of the true nature of God their entire lives through the people they grew up around. You will also meet people who have suffered great trauma at the hands of a person who claimed to be a "Christian." We cannot know every part of a person's story, but God does. He understands every hurt and pain each person is affected by. That is why it is always best to listen to and follow the promptings of the Holy Spirit when talking with anyone. Rushing in with our own words can do more damage than good in a situation where God knows that the best way to bring them to Jesus is to model His patient love in front of them.

The biggest thing I want to convey here is that even in situations where people are hesitant to listen to you, we can't hide our love for Jesus until we feel we've established a close enough relationship with a person to let the cat out of the bag, so to speak. There absolutely will be people who require you to earn their trust before they hear a single word you speak about Jesus. Pain, trauma, and life experiences have a way of building a brick wall over people's hearts. Sometimes evangelism will require us to take the time to remove those bricks one by one with God's help before the truth can truly penetrate the places they have been wounded.

Evangelism will always require the hope of Jesus to be shared, but sometimes the road to get there must be traveled at a slower pace. Because God is love, loving like Him is still effective ministry. We can't let that knowledge trick us into thinking that we can remain silent, love people, and hope they figure out on their on that our love comes from God. Let it spur you on to be completely yielded in speech and action to the movement of the Holy Spirit. He will never prompt you to words too quickly or allow you to remain silent too long.

Jesus calls Himself the light of the world in John 8:12. Then in Matthew 5:14–16, Jesus also says of the ones who choose to follow Him:

> You are the light of the world. A city situated on a hill cannot be hidden. No one lights a lamp and puts it under a basket, but rather on a lampstand, and it gives light for all who are in the house. In the same way, let your light shine before others, so that they may see your good works and give glory to your Father in Heaven.

He has called us to host His light. He has called us to be the light to the darkness of the world by being an example of His love. Light doesn't get to pick and choose who sees its illumination. Light shines wherever it is connected to the source of power. Evangelism is simply accepting the invitation to let the light of Jesus shine wherever you go.

> Jesus came near and said to them, "All authority has been given to me in heaven and on earth. Go, therefore, and make disciples of all nations, baptizing them in the name of the Father and of the Son and of the Holy Spirit, teaching them to observe everything I have commanded you. And remember, I am with you always, to the end of the age." (Matthew 28:18–20 CSB)

These verses from Matthew 28 are known as the Great Commission. This was a charge from Jesus to all who choose to follow Him. We are called to tell people about Jesus, but here we learn that we are also called to make disciples. Nowhere in this commission did Jesus say that only the pastors and seminary graduates were called to make disciples. We are called to be discipled by Jesus and then to go and disciple others. We disciple others by teaching them to observe everything He commanded.

In John 8:31–32, Jesus gives us the standard for being a disciple. He says, "If you continue in my word, you really are my disciples. You will know the truth, and the truth will set you free." Disciples of Jesus live in the Word and by the Word. So if we must live in the Word to be disciples, the way we make disciples is by teaching others to live in the Word as well. This is where the relationship comes in.

Keep in mind, you have no business trying to disciple anyone in the Word of God if you are not a student of God's Word yourself. This does not mean that you must be an expert in every facet of the Bible, only that you must first be actively discipled by Jesus through the Holy Spirit. Remember that the Holy Spirit is also our teacher and will help us gain understanding in the Word. Jesus says in Luke 6:39–40, "Can the blind guide the blind? Won't they both fall into a pit? A disciple is not above his teacher, but everyone who is fully trained will be like his teacher." It is dangerous ground to take someone under your wing when you are not being discipled yourself. You do not have to know all the answers to disciple someone, but you should have the wisdom to inquire of the One who does.

Taking it a step further, it is very wise to be actively discipled by someone you trust who is mature in their faith as well. Timothy is an excellent example of this. He was discipled by Paul as he went to disciple others. Accountability is an undervalued and a much-needed component to the life of a follower of Jesus. Remember, no one who contradicts the Bible should be trusted to speak into your life. The Word is the standard for you to disciple others but also for you to be discipled through.

The goal of discipleship is not to make someone more like you but to be an example of Christ to them. Paul traveled and shared the gospel, but he also was intentional and continued discipling as well. It wasn't enough to Paul only to share the gospel. In Colossians 1:28, Paul says he wanted to continue teaching to present everyone mature in Christ. His letters show the way he did that.

Paul shared the gospel actively. He traveled constantly to reach people in distant places. The New Testament letters Paul penned to specific people and churches were the way he continued teaching and pouring into those whom he ministered to even in his physical absence. In 1 Corinthians 11:1, he tells the Corinthians to imitate him as He imitates Christ. Discipleship is much more than a class or method; it is imitating Christ and coming alongside others as they learn to do the same.

I love the depiction of discipleship found in Acts 18:24–28. Priscilla and Aquila overhear a Jewish man named Apollos speaking in the synagogue. Apollos is passionate in his speech and fervently teaching about Jesus. He was teaching accurately except he only knew of the baptism that John the Baptist taught. He had no knowledge of the baptism that Jesus taught. So Priscilla and Aquila respectfully took him aside to explain the way of God more accurately to him.

Priscilla and Aquila never sought to embarrass Apollos for his error. They didn't begin to refute him in public and start an argument. They gently pulled him away from the crowd to help walk him through the truth. Their actions of discipleship came from a genuine desire to see others know the truth of Jesus rather than a desire to cause shame or appear more enlightened. Because of their loving correction, Apollos went on to be a great help to the disciples and to share the truth with many others.

You cannot teach anyone anything if they are unwilling to learn from you. Speaking into someone's life continually will require trust. Building trust comes with relationship. Jesus called the disciples to follow Him, and as they walked together, they built relationships, which increased their trust in Him. Discipleship is walking together in the Word of God. Walking together requires relationship.

Proverbs 27:17 says, "Iron sharpens iron, and one person sharpens another." We are sharpened by each other. Discipleship doesn't have to look a certain way. It can simply be a weekly phone call to pray and discuss the week's happenings together through the lens of the Bible. It can be a morning sitting on your couch together, drinking coffee, and sharing the scripture on your heart while your kids play. Discipleship can happen around your dining room table while sharing a pizza. On a larger scale, it could be a weekly meeting walking through a book of the Bible with a small group of people.

Some of my favorite stories from the New Testament include Jesus sharing a meal with Lazarus and his sisters. This group had genuine friendship and learned from Jesus as they fellowshipped together.

The most important part of discipleship is growing in the Word of God together. Encourage each other with the Word in times of grief, correct with gentleness in times of wrongdoing, and praise God together when one experiences a victory. As Romans 12:15 reminds us, we weep with those who weep and rejoice with those who rejoice. Pray with and for each other often. I do recommend that couples stick with other couples or women with women and men with men. We still need to be respectful of boundaries and appropriate relationships when spending time with or talking often with another person.

Jesus intended for us to tell others about Him, and He also intended for us to walk together in relationship with other believers. One really incredible occurrence is that oftentimes evangelism can morph into discipleship. I mentioned my friend encouraging a stranger in a parking lot earlier, but I left out one part of the story. She exchanged phone numbers with this person and has been able to keep in touch and encourage her since their initial meeting. A brief encounter opened the door for relationship.

In Matthew 9:37, Jesus says to the disciples, "The harvest is abundant, but the workers are few." The world is hurting and desperate for the hope of Jesus. There are unlimited opportunities to share that hope through evangelism and then cultivate it through discipleship. Later in verse 38, Jesus tells them to pray for workers to be sent out to the harvest. We can join in on that prayer even today.

We can pray for God to raise up people who are unashamed in sharing Jesus Christ, the hope of glory. We can pray that God would make us those workers. I've already written this a few times, but I feel it's important to reiterate here. God will not instruct or command us to do something that He won't empower and help us to do. God will empower you to be ready at any time to share about Jesus to anyone. He will empower and teach you to disciple others. He is faithful. We never have to worry that stepping out in obedience to His Word will leave us stranded. It all starts with allowing Him to disciple you through His Word and the power of His Spirit.

Love is the root of sharing Jesus, whether through evangelism or discipleship, because love is the reason Jesus came to sacrifice Himself for us. The love of God is why we have hope to share. We were first loved by God, and by His love, we can truly love others. In 1 John chapter 4, it is repeated that God is love. True love is a part of God's character. Culture has a different definition of love than God does, and I wanted to finish out this chapter with a look into what real love looks like.

Love is patient, love is kind. Love does not envy, is not boastful, is not arrogant, is not rude, is not self-seeking, is not irritable, and does not keep a record of wrongs. Love finds no joy in unrighteousness but rejoices in the truth. It bears all things, believes all things, hopes all things, endures all things. Love never ends. (1 Corinthians 13:4–8 CSB)

When Jesus said that we will be known as His disciples by our love, this is the kind of love He meant. Love that rejoices in truth while being patient and kind. The love that God claims as part of His own character empowers us to love others without keeping records of their wrongs or boasting. We can't achieve this level of love on our own, but only through the guidance of the Holy Spirit. Pray for these qualities as you go about the business of the kingdom of God.

To bring this full circle, I noticed a significant correlation between how Jesus said we could know we were His disciples and how the world will know we are His disciples. To truly be a disciple of Jesus is to continue in His Word. Disciples of Jesus are students of the Bible but also live out what they learn from it. When we devote ourselves to studying the Scriptures, the Holy Spirit teaches us and empowers us to live out what it calls for. A by-product of living in the Word of God is genuine love, which is how the world will recognize that we know Jesus.

CHAPTER 7

The Evidence of the Holy Spirit in a Person's Life is the Gift of Speaking in Tongues

To preface this chapter: The Bible is clear that the gift of tongues is absolutely an active and current gift of the Holy Spirit. I am not, in any shape, form, or fashion, claiming that speaking in tongues is not evidence of the Holy Spirit within a person; it is. However, the narrative that speaking in tongues is the *only* way to know for certain that you are walking in the Spirit of God is incorrect. There is no biblical proof that every believer of Jesus will or is required to experience this gift.

The argument has become a very denominational one. The confusion on the subject of tongues has done a great deal of damage to the reputation of the Holy Spirit within the church body as a whole and also with unbelievers. On one end of the spectrum, you have churches and individuals who leave the Holy Spirit out of their doctrine altogether because of the mishandling of the gifts of the Spirit by churches and individuals on the complete opposite end of the spectrum. Rather than look at what the Bible says about the Holy Spirit, it's been easier to adopt the all-or-nothing approach.

Claiming false ideas about a part of God is a dangerous game. Sadly, it's not uncommon for "manifestations of the Spirit" to be completely faked to prove one's spirituality. I personally have had conversations with people who were doubting the sincerity of their salvation because they were seeing people speaking in tongues all around them but were unable to do so themselves. It is especially prevalent in the lives of people who spent a great deal of time in church cultures that promoted unbiblical examples of the movement of the Holy Spirit. Not only does this cause doubt to true followers of Jesus, but it can also drive people away from God altogether because of the weirdness and confusion that it brings along with it.

To start our dive into this subject, let's take a look at the gifts of the Holy Spirit that are clearly listed and discussed within the Scriptures. The very first thing we need to understand about the Spirit of God before looking into any of these giftings is that He will never contradict the Word of God or denounce the divinity of Jesus, and neither will the gifts that He brings. God is three-part: Father, Son, and Spirit. John chapter 1 reminds us that the Word is a part of God as well. One part of Himself can never deny or contradict another part of Himself. The giftings of the Holy Spirit are gifts given to us for the purpose of service and building up of the church of Jesus as we learn in 1 Corinthians 14.

> Now there are different gifts, but the same Spirit. There are different ministries, but the same Lord. And there are different activities, but the same God produces each gift in each person. A manifestation of the Spirit is given to each person for the common good: to one is given a message of wisdom through the Spirit, to another, a message of knowledge by the same Spirit, to another, faith by the same Spirit, to another, gifts of healing by the one Spirit, to another, the performing of miracles, to another, prophecy, to another, distinguishing between spirits, to another, different kinds of tongues, to another, interpretation of tongues. One and the same Spirit is active in all these, distributing to each person as he wills. (1 Corinthians 12:4–11 CSB)

The Scriptures give us very clear information in these verses. The Spirit gives gifts to each person as He wills. While the Holy Spirit is absolutely promised to every believer, there is no promise of the gift of tongues being given to every believer. Only the promise that the gifts will be distributed as the Lord sees fit and that they are intended for the common good. We are each sealed by the same Spirit, yet our giftings may not all look the same. Each gift is part of the Spirit who is part of God, and that makes each one excellent.

> For just as the body is one and has many parts, and all parts of that body, though many, are one body—so also is Christ. For we were all baptized by one Spirit into one body—whether Jews or Greeks, whether slaves or free—and we were all given one Spirit to drink. Indeed, the body is not one part but many. If the foot should say, "Because I'm not a hand, I don't belong to the body," it is not for that reason any less part of the body. And if the ear should say, "Because I'm not an eye, I don't belong to the body," it is not for that reason any less a part of the body. If the whole body were an eye, where would the hearing be? If the whole body were an ear, where would the sense of smell be? But as it is, God has arranged each one of these parts in the body just as he wanted. (1 Corinthians 12:12–18 CSB)

I know I'm coming at you with large chunks of scripture so far, but the text does a good job of speaking for itself if we will allow it to. These verses immediately follow the description of the gifts of the Spirit. Instead of thinking in terms of body parts in the last collection of verses, think of it in Spiritual giftings. If every single person had the gift of tongues, where would the miracles be? Where would the wisdom and prophecy be? Each gift is important in building up the church and drawing people to Jesus.

The ear is still a part of the body even though its design doesn't allow it to smell a flower. The ability to hear is just as valuable as the sense of smell. From this description, we can deduce that Paul was telling the Corinthians that not being gifted in a specific area is not proof that you do not belong to the body of Christ. If you have the gift of tongues, it is given by the Spirit. If, however, you don't have the gift of tongues, that is not the standard to which you should judge your inclusion in the body of Christ.

Paul doubles down on this truth in verses 29–31 when he asks, "Are all apostles? Are all prophets? Are all teachers? Do all do miracles? Do all have the gifts of healing? Do all speak in other tongues? Do all interpret? But desire the greater gifts. And I will show you an even better way." Paul was asking rhetorical questions because he knew that not all believers possessed each of these gifts. The body of Christ is diverse in the function of each member as well as the gifts of each member. Paul addresses this diversity within the body of Christ again in Ephesians 4:11–12.

There are a couple of instances in Acts where people receive the Holy Spirit and do immediately speak in tongues. Acts chapter 2 discusses a major encounter of this nature, but we will cover it more thoroughly a little later in this chapter. Another instance is found in Acts chapter 10:44–48 where we find the first account of Gentiles receiving the Holy Spirit. Up until this point, the only people who had received the Spirit were Jews. In the beginning of chapter 10, Peter has a vision in which God tells him not to call anything impure that God has made clean. After this vision, Peter understands that God is clearly stating that Gentiles can now receive the salvation of Jesus along with the Jews.

Here at the end of chapter 10, Peter has preached a message, and these Gentile people believed and received the Holy Spirit. They immediately began speaking in other tongues and declaring the greatness of God. The circumcised, or Jewish, believers who heard this were amazed to see Gentile people receive the Spirit of God. It appears God enabled these Gentiles to demonstrate these giftings to confirm to the Jews that it was, in fact, the same Holy Spirit they had received.

Another instance is found in Acts 19:4–7 where Paul baptizes a group of men who had been disciples of John the Baptist. He laid his hands on these men, and the Holy Spirit came on them. They began to speak in other tongues and also prophesy. Now if we look again at the verses in 1 Corinthians chapter 12 where it teaches that not all will receive the same gifts of the Spirit, why would Paul have written this if every single encounter he had with people receiving the Spirit had included the gift of tongues?

Would you be shocked to learn that Paul didn't experience the gift of tongues when he was first filled with the Holy Spirit? We know from other instances in the Bible that Paul was eventually given the gift of tongues, but his first experience with the Holy Spirit was not through tongues at all. In Acts chapter 9, Paul had encountered Jesus in the form of a voice and a bright light while traveling on the road to Damascus. This light left Paul completely blind for three days. God sends a man named Ananias to meet Paul, who was also known as Saul.

Ananias finds Paul in a house and lays his hands on him. As Paul is filled with the Holy Spirit, the Bible tells us that something like scales fell from his eyes, and his vision was restored. Paul was baptized, and then in verse 20, we learn that Paul immediately began proclaiming Jesus as the Messiah in the synagogues of Damascus. Paul's filling of the Holy Spirit restored his physical sight and empowered him with boldness.

There are other accounts of people receiving the Holy Spirit in the New Testament that do not mention the gift of tongues at all. Just because it happened in a few cases does not mean that it happened in every single one. In fact, we can make the bold assumption that it did not happen in every case because if it had, Paul would have recorded that every person who is baptized in the Holy Spirit should expect to speak in other tongues. Yet Paul himself says that to each is given of the Spirit's will.

Looking again at the last sentence in 1 Corinthians chapter 12, what does Paul mean when he says he will show the Corinthians an even better way? Remember that to fully understand a biblical text, it is wise to read the entire book, especially the chapters preceding and following the selected verse. This is especially helpful in the New Testament books because a majority of them were written as letters to specific people or churches so they would have flowed together without chapter and verse separation. The answer is found in chapter 13 in the very first verse.

> If I speak human or angelic tongues but do not have love, I am a noisy gong or clanging cymbal. If I have the gift of prophecy and understand all mysteries and all knowledge, and if I have all faith so that I can move mountains but do not have love, I am nothing. And if I give away all my possessions, and if I give over my body in order to boast but do not have love, I gain nothing. (1 Corinthians 13:1-3 CSB)

The even better way that Paul spoke of is love. Once again, we find the common denominator with God is the condition of the heart. If you are displaying mighty miracles, healings, various tongues, and prophecy, but the motive is anything but love, these displays are worthless. This theme is probably starting to feel a bit repetitive, but if God addresses it repetitively, then we must understand that it is for a significant purpose. Love that comes from knowing Jesus is unending. Prophecy will end. Tongues will end. Love will remain because our God is love, and He is eternal.

Moving back toward our research on tongues, I think it's important to break down some specifics from the Word about what the gift of tongues is and what its purpose is within the church as a whole. Having a deeper understanding of a subject can relieve the unease that you might be feeling toward it. Throughout the New Testament, there are three types of tongues mentioned: an earthly language, a prayer language or heavenly language, and a message from God with an interpretation. Each differ from one another and have specific functions as we will see.

The first tongue mentioned is found in Acts chapter 2. The disciples were gathered together in Jerusalem during the celebration of Pentecost. At this point in history, Jesus had been crucified, resurrected, and already ascended back to heaven. It is a popular belief that Pentecost started after this outpouring of the Holy Spirit, when in reality, the feast of Pentecost was instated all the way back in Exodus 34. It is also known as the Feast of Weeks or Shavuot. Jerusalem would have been filled with many people from different nations who traveled to celebrate the feast.

As chapter two begins, we see the Holy Spirit come upon these men and women gathered in the upper room together just as Jesus told them He would. A rushing wind filled the house, and tongues like flames of fire appeared and rested on each person present. Then the Holy Spirit filled each one of them, and they all began to speak in different tongues. The word for tongues in this account simply means languages.

The sound of these languages was loud enough that people on the street began to crowd in and listen. In verses 6–7, it says,

> When this sound occurred, a crowd came together and was confused because each one heard them speaking in his own language. They were astounded and amazed saying, "Look, aren't all of these who are speaking Galileans? How is it that each of us can hear them in our own native language?"

It's important to point out that the bystanders' confusion came from their ability to each hear the message in their own languages. They were not confused by the message itself.

Rather than a heavenly language, this particular gifting of tongues created a bridge between these travelers and the disciples through earthly languages. What was the purpose in this incredible encounter? Verse 11 gives us the answer. These foreigners were hearing the disciples proclaim the magnificent works of God in a way that they could understand personally. As the people questioned and mocked, Peter stood and boldly preached his first sermon, one filled with the truth of Jesus and the call to repentance.

It is truly incredible to think of the time line of these events. God, in His complete sovereignty, strategically planned for the Holy Spirit to come to man on this day, at this time, when these nations were gathered in Jerusalem. God brought the nations to the doorstep of the disciples and then equipped them with the languages needed to minister. I'm sure the message of Jesus spread as these people journeyed back home recounting the things they had experienced, so through this encounter, the gospel was taken to the nations.

One more striking tidbit we can glean from this event is further evidence that the Holy Spirit was promised to all who repent and follow Jesus. In Peter's sermon as he calls the hearers to repentance, he says in Acts 2:38–39, "Repent and be baptized, each of you, in the name of Jesus Christ for the forgiveness of your sins, and you will receive the gift of the Holy Spirit. For the promise is for you and for your children, and for all those far off, as many as the Lord will call." We were far off, but by the mercy and grace of our God, we can repent and become sons and daughters of God and carriers of His Holy Spirit!

The second kind of tongues found in the Bible is a prayer language tongue. It is mentioned first in Romans 8:26, where it says, "In the same way the Spirit also helps us in our weakness, because we do not know what to pray for as we should, but the Spirit Himself intercedes for us with unspoken groanings." In the English Standard Version, it refers to the unspoken groanings as groanings too deep for words. This prayer language is mentioned again in 1 Corinthians 14:2: "For the person who speaks in another tongue is not speaking to people but to God, since no one understands him; he speaks mysteries in the Spirit."

Because Paul specifies that this tongue is spoken directly to God, it has no real benefit in the congregational setting. That does not mean to say that this tongue isn't important, only that it is private, between God and the speaker. It is not a tongue that is used to advance the gospel with unbelievers but rather one that allows the Spirit to pray on our behalf when needed. Paul also says in this chapter that we are to pursue these gifts but to especially pursue the gift of prophecy because prophecy builds up the church, whereas tongues build up the speaker.

Prophecy can garner a negative reaction in current times because it has been mishandled just as much as the gift of tongues has. Prophecy is simply a message or word from God. The Bible is full of prophecy, some fulfilled, some awaiting fulfillment; but the biggest thing to remember is that prophecy isn't always a declaration about the future. Paul lists the functions of prophecy in verse 4 of 1 Corinthians chapter 14 as strengthening, encouraging, and consoling to the hearer.

Guess what accomplishes all those things perfectly? The Word of God recorded in the Holy Bible. Any "prophecy" that contradicts the Scriptures or claims to have enlightened knowledge that goes beyond what Scripture says is a false prophecy and should not be given any credibility. Any "thus saith the Lord" statements will back up the things the Lord has already said in His written Word, or it's a "thus saith man" statement.

We took the prophecy rabbit trail to segue into the last type of tongues we will discuss, which is a message with an interpretation. A large portion of 1 Corinthians chapter 14 is dedicated to this type. Paul urges the ones who speak in another tongue to pray that they can also interpret it in verse 13. He goes further to say that if we pray in another tongue, our spirit prays, but our own understanding is unfruitful. Understand that Paul never says we shouldn't desire the ability to pray in the Spirit or sing in the Spirit, only that, without an interpretation, doing so is not beneficial within a congregation or gathering of people.

> The person who prophesies is greater than the person who speaks in tongues, unless he interprets so that the church may be built up. So now, brothers and sisters, if I come to you speaking in other tongues, how will I benefit you unless I speak to you with a revelation or knowledge or prophecy or teaching? Even lifeless instruments that produce sounds—whether flute or harp—if

they don't make a distinction in the notes, how will what is played on the flute or harp be recognized? In fact, if the bugle makes an unclear sound, who will prepare for battle? In the same way, unless you use your tongue for intelligible speech, how will what is spoken be known? For you will be speaking into the air. (1 Corinthians 14:5–9)

Singing in tongues while leading a congregation in worship has become a touchy subject and widely debated topic in the modern church. Paul mentions this specifically in verses 15–17 when he says,

I will sing praise with my spirit, and I will also sing praise with my understanding. Otherwise, if you praise with the spirit, how will the outsider say "Amen" at your giving of thanks, since he does not know what you are saying? For you may very well be giving thanks, but the other person is not being built up.

The goal of meeting together as a church body is to encourage and strengthen each other as believers, but it is also to bring the outsider into an encounter with Jesus. We cannot do that if our behavior within our worship brings more confusion than understanding.

Verse 23 confirms this as Paul says that if an unbeliever enters a church assembly and sees them all speaking in other tongues, the unbeliever will think the entire group has lost their minds. Everything done within the meeting of individual churches is to be done with the unbeliever in mind and with the goal of building up the church. Paul says that prophecy, or speaking God's Word, will draw the unbeliever to repentance and faith in Jesus. As people repent and choose Jesus, the church is built up!

This type of tongues can be used to build up the church, but it requires guidelines and order when used in the congregational setting. Verse 28 tells us that if a person receives a message in tongues, but no one is there to interpret, the person is to keep silent and speak to himself and God. Movements of the Holy Spirit will not put you out of control of your own body or force you into actions that contradict the guidelines laid out for us within the Word. Remember that one of the fruits of the Spirit is self-control. Paul would not tell a person with the gift of tongues to remain silent in this case if the Holy Spirit forced the person into action.

The Holy Spirit can absolutely prompt you to physical action, speech, prayer, song, and many other things in times of worship. However, His promptings will always fall in line with God's Word as we discussed earlier. God's desire is for us to choose to yield to the Spirit in times where He leads to action and in times where He leads to stillness.

Paul tells us in verse 33 that God is a God of order and peace. Chaos is not a characteristic of God, so it is not a characteristic of the Spirit of God. If the Spirit of God is not an author of chaos or confusion, then the people walking in that same Spirit should not be people of chaos or confusion either. God cannot contradict Himself. If you are seeing a contradiction in the way these gifts are handled, the guilty party is the flesh, not God or His Spirit.

With all of this in mind, Paul instructs at the end of the chapter that speaking in other tongues should not be forbidden, only that everything be done in order. In verses 18–19 of chapter 14, Paul says, "I thank God that I speak in other tongues more than all of you; yet in the church I would rather speak five words with my understanding, to teach others also, than ten thousand words in another tongue." Paul agrees that the gift of tongues is a good and beautiful thing, especially when done in the way God intended it.

The confusion and fear that surrounds the topic of this gift specifically in our culture today is proof that when we don't approach congregational worship within the guidelines of the Bible, it makes a mess. When we step outside of what the Word so clearly lays out for us, we open the door for the enemy to lie about the character of our God and cause fear. I am saddened knowing that there are people who completely discount the beneficial and good gifts of the Holy Spirit because of the way humans have handled it.

I can't help but think back to the account of Uzzah in 1 Chronicles chapter 13. King David had gathered Israel to bring the Ark of the Covenant back home among God's people. We touched on this in an earlier chapter, but remember that the Ark of the Covenant was placed in the holiest part of the sanctuary where the presence of God resided. Only the priest could enter. The Levites were given very specific instructions on how the Ark was to be handled, packed up, and carried as the Israelites traveled with it in the wilderness. The Ark was to be picked up by long poles so that no one touched the actual Ark as they moved.

As the procession moved through with the Ark resting in a cart driven by oxen, the oxen stumbled. Uzzah was one of the men guiding the cart, and as the oxen stumbled, he reached out to touch the Ark, and he immediately died. I know that sounds incredibly harsh, but God gave them specific instructions about its care for a reason. The Ark was holy, and man was still living in sin that required a blood sacrifice. Holiness and unatoned sin cannot occupy the same space. The instructions were there to protect the people.

God cares deeply about how His presence is handled. That is the reason He made sure we were left with specific instructions on how to behave and represent the Spirit of God. When we, as humans always do, take it into our own hands and act from our preference or tradition rather than what the truth of the Word says, it always comes with consequences. Just like Jesus warned the Pharisees in Mark chapter 7 by quoting from Isaiah, teaching human traditions and commands as doctrine is disobedience, and disobedience never glorifies God.

After looking more deeply at the gifts of the Spirit and tongues specifically, we can say with certainty that those giftings can absolutely be evidence of the Holy Spirit at work in your life. However, the Bible also lists other qualities and characteristics that should be a part of anyone who is walking in the Spirit of God. Galatians 5 teaches about what it looks like to walk in the Spirit verses walking in the flesh.

> But the fruit of the Spirit is love, joy, peace, patience, kindness, goodness, faithfulness, gentleness, and self-control. The law is not against such things. Now those who belong to Christ have crucified the flesh with its passions and desires. If we live by the Spirit, let us also keep in step with the Spirit. (Galatians 5:22–25 CSB)

When you are walking in step with the Spirit, these qualities will become evident in your life. Whereas gifts are given at the expense of the giver, fruit is grown by preparation, care, time, and work. The fruit of the Spirit will grow as we make the conscious choice to daily yield to God and His Spirit. You are producing fruit whether you are walking in the Spirit or not, and the fruit you produce will either proclaim the identity of Christ or the identity of the flesh. As we learn earlier in Galatians 5, the works, or fruits, of the flesh are sexual immorality, moral impurity, promiscuity, idolatry, sorcery, hatred, strife, jealousy, outbursts of anger, selfish ambitions, dissensions, factions, envy, drunkenness, carousing, and anything similar.

In Matthew 7:16, as He is warning about false prophets, Jesus states that people will be recognized by their fruit. The Greek word used for fruit in Matthew chapter 7 is the exact same word used for fruit in Galatians chapter 5. The evidence of the Holy Spirit working in your life is bearing fruit that possesses the characteristics of the Spirit of God. It's very simple. Just like a pear tree must produce pears, a person filled with the Spirit of God must produce fruit that is indicative of the Spirit.

As Jesus was preparing to ascend back to heaven after His resurrection, He tells the disciples of the coming Holy Spirit in Acts chapter 1. In verse 8, Jesus tells them that they will receive power when the Holy Spirit comes so that they could go boldly declaring the gospel to the world around them. We get an incredible picture of this boldness in the life of Peter. Peter denied that He knew Jesus three times while Jesus was on trial to be crucified. His fear of the repercussions he could face from admitting that he followed Jesus was too heavy to shake.

After the Holy Spirit came, Peter became empowered with boldness like never before as we see him preach to crowds completely unashamed. All through Acts, we see these Spirit-filled disciples go and boldly speak about Jesus and perform signs and miracles. Their boldness was unfazed by beatings, imprisonment, and even the threat of death. There is no other explanation for this drastic change other than the power of the Holy Spirit working within them.

In Acts chapter 4, Peter and John were arrested by the temple police and Sadducees for speaking about Jesus after they had healed a lame man. The text tells us that many who heard their message believed. While on trial, the high priest asked Peter and John by what power they had done this. Peter, filled with the Holy Spirit, began to declare the power of Jesus even there in the presence of men who were capable of imprisoning him or having him killed.

In verse 13, we learn that the boldness of Peter and John is what proved to the Sanhedrin that these men had truly been with Jesus. Peter and John were uneducated and untrained, yet the boldness they spoke and acted with was undeniable. Unable to find a reason to punish them further, the Sanhedrin released Peter and John with the charge to stop speaking about Jesus, which of course, they refused. In verse 20, they said that they were unable to stop speaking about what they had seen and heard.

They had encountered the power of God in such miracu-lous ways that they couldn't keep their testimonies hidden away. Immediately after they were released, they joined their own people again and began to declare praises to God and pray for even more boldness. Notice that they didn't ask for more tongues or prophecy or even miracles, not that asking God for those gifts is wrong; they fully understood that boldness was a great advantage in sharing the gospel. The power of the Holy Spirit creates boldness in those who are filled with the Spirit!

In Ezekiel 36:27, God is speaking about how He will restore the people of Israel and says, "I will place my Spirit within you and cause you to follow my statutes and carefully observe my ordinances." Jesus says in John 16:13 that the Spirit will guide us into all truth. Again, in John chapter 14, Jesus says that the Holy Spirit will teach us all things and bring His words to our remembrance. The Holy Spirit brings understanding of the Word of God and also empowers us to live out what we learn. In other words, if there is a constant public display of spiritual giftings with no visible obedience to the Word of God, it is very likely that it is not the Spirit of God who is orchestrating the giftings.

> Now the Lord is the Spirit, and where the Spirit of the Lord is, there is freedom. We all, with unveiled faces, are looking as in a mirror at the glory of the Lord and are being transformed into the same image from glory to glory; this is from the Lord who is the Spirit. (2 Corinthians 3:17–18)

God's Spirit is so much more than a gift giver. He is what empowers us to become Christlike. He teaches us and comforts us. He corrects us and kindly leads us to repentance. He brings wisdom and understanding. He helps us walk in joy and hope and then gives us the boldness to share the reason for our hope. He helps us love our enemies and pray for them. He prays on our behalf when we can't muster words. He ushers us into the freedom that comes from Jesus. Jesus was serious when He said that it was to our benefit that He went away so that the Spirit could come to us.

Jesus asks in Luke 11:13, "If you then, who are evil, know how to give good gifts to your children, how much more will the heavenly Father give the Holy Spirit to those who ask him?" The Holy Spirit is the good gift. Just like Peter and the disciples, who were already filled with the Holy Spirit, asked for even more boldness, you can ask for more of the Holy Spirit as well. Personally, I have made it a priority to ask God for every good gift He has planned for me. Ask God for more of His Spirit. Ask Him to show you the areas in your life that are proof of the Holy Spirit working within you.

The Holy Spirit that fills you with beneficial giftings is the same Spirit that will help you understand the way the Word calls for those giftings to be handled. Don't buy into the lie that you have to speak in other tongues, or you aren't truly following Jesus. The Holy Spirit is God's seal on you as a follower of Jesus and the down payment on your inheritance. His gifts are good and have purpose. His companionship and guidance are available. Get to know God through His Word, and you will get to know the Holy Spirit more intimately as well.

CHAPTER 8

ALL WE CAN DO NOW IS PRAY

All people crave control to some extent. I really believe it's part of our human nature to want to feel like we have a tight rein on all aspects of our lives. As we age, it becomes more apparent that we simply cannot control everything. Outside factors cause problems that are unavoidable. Sicknesses and diseases infect our bodies. Accidents occur. Mistakes happen even for the most diligent people. Life unfolds speedily and sometimes unexpectedly.

We desperately try everything in our power to right wrongs. We see all the specialists, take all the medicines, follow all the recommendations, but sometimes it simply isn't enough. Desperate circumstances have a way of grabbing our attention and reverting our focus back to the power of God. When things happen that are out of our control, we suddenly realize how little power we have in our flesh to truly change the situations we find ourselves in. This place of desperation is typically where people make the statement that "all we can do now is pray."

Bringing your heart to God out of desperation is not wrong. He cares for us and asks to take our burdens. Psalm 34:18 says of God that He is "close to the brokenhearted; he saves those crushed in spirit." David says in Psalm 51:17 that God will not despise a broken and humbled heart. And we can't forget our key scripture from the very first chapter where Paul says, in 1 Corinthians 12, that God's power is perfected in our weakness.

By all means, cry out to God when you are hurt or angry. Bring your heartache to the God of comfort. Place in His hand those problems that have no earthly solution anywhere in sight. Prayer is powerful! The power of prayer is the exact reason I chose to include this specific quote in this book. Prayer is too powerful to be considered a last resort. Prayer is too powerful to be the last option on the list of possible solutions.

It is human nature to search for solutions on our own, but as followers of Jesus, we no longer operate in human nature. By repenting and choosing to live for Jesus, the Holy Spirit is placed within you so that you now have the ability to operate in the Spirit of God! Because of the Spirit of God at work within us, the news that there are parts of life we have no control over isn't devastating anymore. We now intimately know the One has control and dominion over everything! Not only do we know Him, but we have unlimited and unhindered access to Him. The last few verses of Hebrews chapter 4 refer to Jesus as our great high priest who can sympathize with our weakness. In verse 16, it says, "Therefore, let us approach the throne of grace with boldness, so that we may receive mercy and find grace to help us in time of need." Prayer is powerful because of who we pray to!

Prayer is so much more than a formality for us. It is a lifeline, but if we don't fully understand the power in it, it's easy for it to take a back seat in our daily lives until tragedy strikes. Fortunately for us, the Bible is not silent on the subject of prayer. We can learn so much about its impact from Old Testament accounts, the ministry of the disciples, and even Jesus's time on earth.

Did you know that Jesus is praying and interceding for you at the right hand of God? In 1 Timothy 2:5, Jesus is referred to as the mediator between God and humanity. In His time on earth, Jesus modeled a life of prayer. Throughout the gospels, we see Him take time away to pray often. If the Son of God made it a point to pray consistently, we must realize that a lifestyle of prayer is an absolute necessity for us as believers as well.

He was praying in a certain place, and when
he finished, one of his disciples said to him,

"Lord, teach us to pray, just as John also taught
his disciples." (Luke 11:1 CSB)

The disciples took note of the way Jesus prayed because it was a
sight they witnessed often. Jesus put such emphasis on prayer in his
teachings and in the way He lived that the disciples obviously recognized that prayer must be a powerful thing. In a culture that empha-
sized reciting prayers, they must have realized there was something
different about the way Jesus prayed. I love that the disciples first
asked Jesus to teach them how to pray. I genuinely think there are
believers in Jesus all over the world who don't pray, not because they
question its power but because they don't truly understand how to
pray. It's one thing to bow your head as your pastor prays in a church
service. It's an entirely different ball game when you are responsible
for coming up with the words to say to the King of the universe.

I know people who pray in response to everything, whether
good or bad. I also know people who love Jesus but struggle with
even praying a short blessing over their meal. It's easy to assume that
prayer is natural for all followers of Jesus when that just isn't the case.
It can be intimidating or awkward. Shame can creep in and try to
convince you that your past failures make you unworthy to speak to
God or that your limited "church vocabulary" is inadequate to get
the job done. I've even caught myself neglecting to pray out of fear
that my cares were too minute to bother God with.

It is incredible to me that the disciples felt so comfortable with
Jesus that they unashamedly asked for a lesson on prayer. Even the
men who physically walked with Jesus needed a better understanding of it. Please don't feel embarrassed or ashamed if prayer is intimidating to you. Jesus never made the disciples feel less because they
had questions. He took the time to teach His disciples, and now we
can glean, all these years later, from that lesson as well.

Whenever you pray, you must not be like
the hypocrites, because they love to pray standing in the synagogues and on the street corners
to be seen by people. Truly I tell you, they have

their reward. But when you pray, go into your private room, shut your door, and pray to your Father who is in secret. And your Father who sees in secret will reward you. When you pray, don't babble like the Gentiles, since they imagine they'll be heard for their many words. Don't be like them, because your Father knows the things you need before you ask him. (Matthew 6:5–8 CSB)

The very first thing we should notice from this text is the wording of the first sentence. Jesus says *whenever* we pray, not *if* we pray. Prayer is to be a normal part of a life that is surrendered to Jesus. Prayer is a foundational part of our faith rather than an optional or conditional one. As we've seen many other times on this journey through the Word, Jesus was once again addressing a heart issue all while teaching about prayer. Jesus is not instructing us to only pray in private. We will see examples of public and corporate prayer as we walk through more biblical examples, but here, Jesus is first pointing to the posture of the heart as we pray. As with every other aspect of our faith, God desires for our hearts to be motivated to pray for the right reasons.

A prayer life that is cultivated and developed with intimacy is one that will spill out into the culture around you. Luke 5:16 tells us that Jesus often withdrew from the crowds and His disciples and went to deserted places to pray. A lasting devotion to God will be sustained by the times you spend in conversation, or prayer, with God in private. A marriage would have very little chance of lasting if a husband and wife only ever spoke to each other in public settings. A relationship with God is similar in that aspect. God is reminding us once again that He sees the hidden places in a person; He sees the heart. Public devotion to prayer to be seen means very little to God.

God values our prayers, but He does not value prideful prayers. Jesus paints a picture of prayer that is motivated by selfish desires and vanity as an example of how not to come before God. Praying with the intent to impress people in the room with you is not a prayer truly offered to God. Heaping up phrases filled with church lingo to give the appearance of holiness is not a prayer truly offered to God. Just as we discovered looking into handling our money, our motivation matters.

God is not impressed by eloquent speeches; He is moved by a heart that is devoted to Him. If you struggle finding the words to pray, let this fact be encouragement to you: your devotion to Jesus will speak eloquently enough on its own without beautifully packaged prayers. Jesus even reminds us of that when He says, "Your Father knows the things you need before you ask him." He desires to hear from you, but you don't have to fret that your words don't adequately relay what you need. Your Father already knows.

After Jesus gives these examples, He lays out a guideline for prayer:

> Therefore, you should pray like this: Our Father in heaven, your name be honored as holy. Your kingdom come. Your will be done on earth as it is in heaven. Give us today our daily bread. And forgive us our debts, as we also have forgiven our debtors. And do not bring us into temptation, but deliver us from the evil one. (Matthew 6:9–13 CSB)

This guideline for prayer isn't a script meant to be replicated word for word every time you call on the Lord. Please don't think that God only hears us when we pray these words exactly. This outline was given to us as a starting point for praying. There will be times when your prayers are so specific and flow easily from your being. It is completely okay to pray specifically to God.

There will also be times when you struggle to find the strength to get a sentence out. We will look deeper into those subjects as well. This outline is an example of a prayer that covers all the bases. Remember that order is important. They way this prayer is laid out shows the order in which our priorities should be set in prayer and also in our hearts.

Our first priority should always be thanking and giving glory to God. He is the One we pray to and the One who is in control of everything we are facing. He is our Father and King. He is worthy of praise always. In good seasons and bad alike, His goodness and worthiness does not waver or change. Praising Him is a constant in the life of a believer because He is constantly worthy. Going further, the statement "Your kingdom come" is a direct acknowledgment of God's power and authority. It is a recognition of the fact that God's kingdom is the true authority and holder of your allegiance.

Asking for God's will to be done signifies the surrender of your own will. When you surrender to God's will, you agree that the Lord's plans are greater than your own. It is the ultimate declaration of trust to come before God with your most pressing concerns and ask for His will in the situation over your own. Surrendering to His will is essentially releasing the reins and removing your hands from the circumstance. We surrender to God and ask Him to align our perspectives here on earth with heaven's perspective.

The very next line "Give us today our daily bread" shows why we can trust Him enough to surrender. He cares enough to sustain us through each day. His plans are for good, and if we can trust Him with our daily sustenance, we can surely trust Him even in dire situations. Notice that Jesus only mentions bread for the day. We aren't expected to fret over the past or anxiously ponder on how we will survive in the coming days. We can focus on one day at a time because our Father knows what we need. He's already covered your past with His blood, and He's already seen ahead into tomorrow.

We should always come before God with a repentant heart. Repentance is what begins our relationship with Jesus, but it isn't a one-time occasion for a follower of Jesus. Remember, we are flesh, and so our struggle with sin still exists even after salvation. As you walk with the Spirit of God and study the Word, God's kindness will lead you to repentance over and over. As we receive forgiveness, we should be constantly releasing forgiveness as well. God wants us to come before Him with no grudges against anyone. Forgiveness is a quality of God, and we, as His children, get the opportunity to extend forgiveness as well.

The very last line in the Lord's prayer is a reminder to us that God will guide and protect us. We can trust Him with our biggest and smallest problems. We can trust that His plans are for good and will come to pass. We can trust Him to sustain us. We can trust Him to forgive us and empower us to forgive others. We can trust Him to be our Shepherd. We can trust Him with our prayers for all of those things.

> "I pray not only for these, but also for those who believe in me through their word. May they all be one, as you, Father, are in me and I am in you. May they also be in us, so that the world may believe you sent me." (John 17:20–21 CSB)

These verses were prayed by Jesus in the garden of Gethsemane right before He was arrested. He begins by praying for Himself, asking that God would glorify Him so that God would be glorified in the process. He then prays for His disciples. He prayed for them to be sanctified by the truth of God's Word. To conclude His prayer, He prays for us, the ones who would come to know Jesus through the ministry of the disciples. Before Jesus shed His blood on the cross, He prayed for you. Facing the most terrifying and painful thing His human body would ever experience, He prayed *first*.

Jesus knew exactly what fate awaited Him. He was so grieved in His spirit that, as Luke 22:44 tells us, he began to sweat drops of blood as His prayer increased fervently. I cannot imagine the turmoil He felt, yet as He prayed, He surrendered to God's will before any other action was taken. In Luke 22:42, He prays, "Father, if you are willing, take this cup away from me—nevertheless, not my will, but yours, be done." Jesus, the Son of God, modeled an example of prayer as the first response followed by complete surrender to the will of the Father, even knowing what God's will held for Him.

> The Lord is near. Don't worry about anything, but in everything, through prayer and petition with thanksgiving, present your requests

to God. And the peace of God, which surpasses
all understanding, will guard your hearts and
minds in Christ Jesus. (Philippians 4:5–7 CSB)

Paul gives us instruction in these verses to pray about *everything*.
No request is too large or too small to be presented to God. Any
situation that causes you to worry or be anxious is worth submitting to God. Remember, the Word of God won't instruct us to do
anything that God, through His Word and His Spirit, is incapable
of empowering us to do. If God inspired Paul to write to the church
to exchange worry for peace through prayer, He meant it. When we
cast our cares into the hands of our conquering, mighty, all-powerful
King, peace is the supernatural result.

1 Thessalonians 5:17 tells us to pray constantly, or as some
translations put it, without ceasing. We know that it is physically
impossible to pray every single moment of every single day. Our bodies require sleep, activity, and nourishment. Our jobs and families
require our focus and attention. God knows and understands this.
Praying constantly means that prayer is our first response in every
circumstance. When we are afraid or unnerved, when we are joyous
and thankful, when we are uncertain of the future or overwhelmed
by the past, the response should be the same—pray. Prayer can be
in the form of praise and thanksgiving in the same way it can be for
survival and rescue.

After we are instructed to pray constantly in 1 Thessalonians
5:17, verse 18 puts it all into even greater perspective. It says of constant prayer, thanksgiving, and rejoicing, that this is God's will for us
in Christ Jesus! God's will for us is that we devote ourselves to prayer.
Prayer is not a suggestion; it is a way of life! Jesus modeled this for us
in the flesh because He is the Word made flesh. Remember that disciples begin to act and look like their teacher, and praying constantly
is one way that we begin to look like Jesus.

Oh, the depth of the riches both of the
wisdom and of the knowledge of God! How
unsearchable his judgements and untraceable

his ways! For who has known the mind of the
Lord? Or who has been his counselor? And who
has ever given to God, that he should be repaid?
For from him and through him and to him are
all things. To him be the glory forever. Amen.
(Romans 11:33–36 CSB)

I mentioned earlier that God can be trusted to sustain us. What
makes God trustworthy with our deepest cares and concerns? Why
would we trust Him with the people and situations that we most
want to protect? There is no greater wisdom or understanding than
God's. All things are from Him. All things are seen by Him. All
things are completely understood by Him. He created the human
body, so He knows exactly how diseases affect it. He fashioned every
bone and filled every lung with His own breath. He is aware of every
cell.

God knows the human heart because He sees every aspect of
each emotion and thought. He understands your desires and devotions even more intimately than you do. He knows every family
dynamic because He formed each member in their mother's womb.
There are no personalities that are a mystery to Him. He is outside
of time, so He knows every detail of your past and sees every second
of your future, all while being completely present in what you are
experiencing in this very moment.

On a larger scale, He created the world and everything in it.
Politics aren't outside of His vision. The dynamics in play between
countries aren't hidden to Him. All the hidden agendas are fully
seen and known by Him. As cliché as it may sound, He really does
have the world, in its entirety, in His hands. He doesn't miss one
single thing. He isn't so consumed with your daily grievances that
He missed the cancer diagnosis in another family, and He isn't so
wrapped up in the major political happenings that He doesn't notice
your broken heart.

When the psalmist says in Psalm 121:2 that his help comes
from the Lord, the Maker of heaven and earth, it is such a sobering
thought to dwell on. He made everything and everyone my eyes can

see, and yet He comes to help *me*? Going further in Psalm 121, verses 3–4 tell us that God doesn't sleep or slumber. The text calls Him the Protector of Israel. We are grafted in with Israel as His children now because of Jesus. God classifies Himself as our ever-aware Protector.

God knowing, seeing, and understanding everything He made is incredible and a little mind-blowing to process. Yet knowing that God is omniscient isn't the only reason He is trustworthy with our prayers. His authority and power have no match on the earth or in heaven. There is nothing and no one that can come against His plans and succeed. Ephesians 3:20 tells us that He is able to do above and beyond what we ask or think. As we mentioned in a previous chapter, after God spoke to Job about His power and authority, Job responded in verse 2 of chapter 42, "I know that you can do anything and no plan of yours can be thwarted."

God asks us to trust Him, and He has the sovereign power to justify our trust. There is no problem too great for Him. Even the enemy can't stand against His Word and authority. The wind and waves bow to Him. The sun stands still at His command. The ocean's tide stops in the exact place He created for it. Every organ system contained in our bodies must submit to His instruction. There isn't a single scenario that you could present to God that He doesn't have the ultimate authority over, and because He is good and fair, there is no greater comfort than that fact.

God is the truest definition of good. Psalm 34:8 invites us to taste and see for ourselves that He is, in fact, good. Romans 8:28 says, "We know that all things work together for the good of those who love God, who are called according to his purpose." If God is good and He works out everything for good, we can trust that His will is good. If you have submitted your life to Jesus through repentance and received His salvation, you are one of those called according to His purpose. Those things in life that are terrifying, devastating, and heartbreaking, He promises to work them for the ultimate good.

In Genesis chapters 37–50, we find the account of Joseph's life. Joseph was the beloved son of Jacob or Israel as God later renamed him. Israel had other sons who were jealous of Joseph and their father's love for him. Their jealousy eventually led them to sell Joseph into slavery in Egypt. God gave Joseph the ability to interpret dreams, which ultimately led to him being promoted from a prisoner to being second in command over the land of Egypt during a time of plenty followed by a great famine across the entire land.

Because of Joseph's God-given gift and wisdom, he counseled Pharaoh in making preparations for the coming seven-year famine, and Egypt had plenty of food to sell to other lands who had not fared as well. Joseph's brothers eventually came to purchase food. They did not recognize Joseph because so many years had passed, but Joseph recognized them. There is a great deal more to the story, which I encourage you to read for yourself, but the part I want to highlight is found in Genesis 50:20 after Joseph had forgiven his brothers and moved them and his father to Egypt to continue providing for them. Joseph says in verse 19, "Don't be afraid. Am I in the place of God? You planned evil against me; God planned it for good to bring about the present result—the survival of many people."

Joseph had to walk through so many trials. He had to live with the betrayal of his family that led him to a seemingly hopeless place through no fault or choice of his own, but through it all, he saw the way God took the evil things done to him and worked them out for not only his own personal good, but for the good of thousands of people who survived the famine. Even the evil done to you at the hand of another person is no match for the goodness and plans of God. We can trust Him because His plan will always be for good, and it will always prevail.

Looking back on what we have covered so far, we know that it is God's will for us to live a lifestyle of prayer, just like Jesus did, and that God is worthy to receive our prayers. Now we must discover what happens in the physical and spiritual realms when we pray. First, we need to understand that our prayers are important to God. In Revelation chapter 5, John is seeing a vision of the throne room of heaven. In verse 8, he describes the four living creatures falling down in worship before Jesus as He takes a scroll to open it. Each living creature holds a harp and golden bowls filled with incense.

Revelation can be confusing because of the amount of symbolism that is used, but John offers a very specific definition of the incense contained in the golden bowls in this account. At the end of verse 8, he specifies that the incense is the prayers of the saints. The saints referred to here are the people who are redeemed by and devoted to Jesus. Your prayers are so precious to God that they are used as incense in the throne room of heaven. I have heard people say in frustration that they felt their prayers were only reaching the ceiling of their house. Here is biblical proof that our prayers reach much further than we could ever imagine.

Did you know that burning incense was a requirement in the temple before Jesus came? Only the priests were able to carry the burning censers into the sanctuary, but it was another type of offering that was made to the Lord. The incense was burned daily. In Exodus 30, God gave Moses a specific, holy recipe for how it was to be made. It was a fragrant incense. We see throughout the Old Testament where God says of the sacrifices offered that they are a pleasing aroma to Him.

Your prayers are valuable enough to God to be considered a pleasing aroma and to be acknowledged as such in His very throne room. Don't miss that the incense in the temple was burned daily and regularly. It was not an occasional offering. The incense was offered by the priests regularly in times of good and times of bad. Now, as we learn in 1 Peter 2:9, we who follow Jesus are called a royal priesthood. We can now approach the throne of God with our incense of prayer and should do so daily!

We can't overlook the fact that prayer is what begins our walk with God through salvation. Romans 10:9 says, "If you confess with your mouth, 'Jesus is the Lord,' and believe in your heart that God raised him from the dead, you will be saved." 1 John 1:9 tells us, "If we confess our sins, he is faithful and righteous to forgive us our sins and to cleanse us from all unrighteousness." Conversation with God, or prayer, is how we confess our sins and our devotion. If we can be certain of our salvation and eternal promise being secured through prayer, we can surely rely on it amidst earthly, temporary trials.

All throughout the Psalms, you will find verses that show the psalmist crying out to God and then praising God because He heard each cry. In 1 John 5:14–15, it says, "This is the confidence we have before him: if we ask anything according to his will, he hears us. And if we know that he hears whatever we ask, we know that we have what we have asked of him." When we pray in the manner Jesus laid out for us in the Lord's prayer, we pray in accordance with God's will, and when we pray in His will, He promises to hear us! Again, Jesus reminds us of the importance of devotion in John 15:7 when He says, "If you remain in me and my words remain in you, ask whatever you want and it will be done for you." We cannot abide in Him without His Word, and His Word teaches us how to pray in God's will.

James chapter 5 speaks on prayer a great deal, and in it, James tells us that the prayer of a righteous person has great power. To be righteous means to be in right standing with God. The Lord's prayer lays out the attitude of the righteous person: one who is redeemed by the blood of Jesus, repents, forgives, and submits to the will of God. James also tells us that the prayer of faith can save a sick person and highlights the importance of praying corporately over a person who is sick or suffering.

In verses 17–18, James gives the example of Elijah praying earnestly for God to hold back the rain, and for three years, there was no rain. When Elijah prayed again for rain to come, the Lord brought rain, and in turn, God's power and glory were demonstrated. You can read Elijah's account in 1 Kings 17–19. Elijah was a regular human who submitted to the authority, Word, and will of God, and through his obedience, God did miraculous things.

Looking back to James, in chapter 1 verse 5, he says that if anyone lacks wisdom, he can ask God for it. He even specifies that God gives wisdom generously and ungrudgingly. In Jeremiah 33:3, God tells Jeremiah to call out to Him, and He will tell him great and incomprehensible things. I love seeing the way the Holy Spirit confirms the Scriptures, and here we have another instance of that. When we ask for wisdom, it's the Holy Spirit who comes in to teach us. When we pray, it doesn't negate the Holy Spirit's job; it facilitates it!

Take the helmet of salvation and the sword
of the Spirit—which is the word of God. Pray

at all times in the Spirit with every prayer and request, and stay alert with all perseverance and intercession for all the saints. (Ephesians 6:17–18 CSB)

The verses above are the last part of the description of the armor of God that we are to dress ourselves in as we face spiritual warfare. Here, we are instructed not only to pray, but to pray in the Spirit at all times. Romans 8:26 reminds us that when we are unable to pray as we should, the Spirit takes over for us with groanings too deep for words. Those times where you feel the words just won't come, pray anyway. The Holy Spirit is prepared to pray what He knows needs to be said.

God is not separate from His Spirit, and He proves that once again in His provisions for us as we pray through hard things. While praying in a prayer language or tongue is absolutely a way to pray in the Spirit, praying in the Spirit doesn't just entail praying with a heavenly language. We know that the Holy Spirit confirms God's Word and honors God's will. When we pray that God's will would be done here on earth in the same way it is in heaven, that is praying in the Spirit as well!

One other beautiful confirmation we can take from these verses is further proof that God is not separate from His Word, and neither is His Spirit. Our defense in the battle is the sword of the Spirit, and these verses clarify that the Word of God is that sword. Did you know that there is power is praying the Word of God? The Word lacks nothing. If God called it our weapon—the only weapon included in our armor—we cannot underestimate the power held within it. Hebrews 4:12 says that the Word of God is alive and effective and sharper than any double-edged sword. It also says that the Word is able to penetrate the separation of soul and spirit, joints and marrow, and judge the intentions of the heart and mind.

The last few words of Ephesians 6:18 encourage us to intercede for the saints. Interceding for the saints simply means to pray for other believers all around the world. Prayer is another way that the church is unified across the globe. In Acts, the disciples modeled this often. Paul frequently asked for the churches receiving his letters to continually pray for him and the ministry he was doing. Galatians 6:2 encourages us to bear one another's burdens. It is an honor that we get to pray for our brothers and sisters.

Many times in Acts, we find it stated that the disciples met together and were devoted to and unified through prayer. In Matthew 18:19–20, Jesus says, "Again, truly I tell you, if two of you on earth agree about any matter that you pray for, it will be done for you by my Father in heaven. For where two or three are gathered together in my name, I am there among them." Jesus prayed in John chapter 17 that all of His followers would be one, just as He is one with the Father. Uniting in prayer is one way that we can see that oneness become a reality. Unity among the body of Christ is beautiful on its own, but I love that Jesus promises to be among us when we join together in fellowship and agreement.

In Acts chapter 12, Herod had begun attacking followers of Jesus. He had James, Jesus's brother, executed. The Bible tells us that these attacks and executions pleased the Jews, so Herod arrested Peter as well with the intention to bring him out to be executed during the Festival of Unleavened Bread. While Peter was locked away under the guard of four squads of soldiers, the church was united and fervently praying to God on behalf of Peter.

On the very night that Herod planned to bring Peter out to trial, an angel of the Lord appeared within the cell. Not only was Peter locked in a cell, but he was doubly bound with chains, sleeping in between two guards, and watched by two more guards at the door. The angel woke Peter, and the chains fell off him. The angel then escorted Peter out of the prison without being detected. Prayer aligns us with God's will, and things happen when the church unites in prayer that honors God!

Prayer makes a difference in the world all around us. I have seen miraculous things happen when people come together under the banner of the name of Jesus and pray that the will of God would be done. Paul urges believers in 1 Timothy 2:1–2 to pray for the leadership in authority over you. This includes, but isn't limited to, presidents, governors, mayors, and even your employer or manager.

He goes on to say in verse 3, "This is good, and it pleases God our Savior, who wants everyone to be saved and come to the knowledge of truth." Whether you agree with or even understand the politics in play or not, you are equipped to pray for the salvation of people in places of authority. God desires everyone to come to Him, and He wouldn't waste time asking us to pray if it made no difference.

Loving and praying for people you are close with is easy. Loving and praying for brothers and sisters in Christ that you've never met is probably relatively simple to you too. It becomes a little more challenging when you find the charge to pray for people whom you disagree with, such as political rulers. Did you know that Jesus takes it a step further in Matthew 5:44 and instructs us to love and pray for our enemies who persecute us?

In Romans 12:14–21, Paul reminds us to repay evil with good and bless our enemies. He quotes Proverbs 25:21–22, which says that doing so will heap burning coals on the head of your enemy. The burning coal can be interpreted as punishment, as it sometimes symbolizes the judgment of God. However, fire and burning coals were also used in some cases to represent the refinement that comes from God. Blessing your enemies through love and prayer leaves room for God to take responsibility for their judgment, rather than you and may even open the door for that person to allow God to refine them and their actions.

> Honor his holy name; let the hearts of those who seek the Lord rejoice. Seek the Lord and his strength; seek his face always. (1 Chronicles 16:10–11 CSB)

Prayer is powerful because God is powerful. The scriptures covered in this chapter relating to prayer are just skimming the surface. I could fill pages with verses that mention prayer or encourage us to pray, but the truth is, you will never fully understand the power in prayer until you discover it for yourself. Take the challenge to become someone who prays first. Start a prayer journal if that will help you create a habit. Write down every prayer that you want to hand over to God. Ask the Holy Spirit to remind you of prayer throughout the day.

You can also ask Him to highlight situations and people throughout your daily life that you should pray for. Practice going to the Lord, asking Him to help you align your will to His will. Pray the Word of God. When the inclination to pray becomes natural in the more trivial experiences and troubles, it will also become like second nature to go immediately to prayer in the desperate ones as well.

Private prayer between you and God cannot be neglected. Your relationship with God cannot be deepened without it. Your husband or wife cannot bring you into a closer relationship with God through their intimacy with God. What we sow into the relationship will determine how closely we walk with God, just as it is in every human relationship you hold. However, there is an undeniable bond of unity that comes from a husband and wife praying in one accord. Genesis 2:24 tells us that a man leaves his parents, is joined with his wife, and they become one flesh. Remember Jesus said that where two or more come together in agreement, He is among them. If you are not praying with your spouse regularly, you are missing a beautiful and powerful connection.

Husbands, you are the head of your household. Don't sit back and wait on your wife to ask you to lead. Take the charge given to you by God and ignite a fire for the Lord in your home beginning with praying together. Let your children hear your voice pray. There is no better example of biblical leadership and masculinity in your home than to gather your family to pray when facing the hills and valleys of life. Wives, submit to your husband and encourage and pray for him to be the leader whom God designed him to be.

As Joshua decreed in Joshua 24:15, you must make the conscious choice to lead your family to worship the Lord. You must make the choice personally before you can ever lead your family in His ways. You cannot lead someone to a place you refuse to go for yourself. Lead by action that matches your words. Let your priorities be known in the tone of your life rather than just the tone of your voice. That choice, just like many others, can be ignited by a prayer of surrender.

You cannot sustain a healthy prayer life by your own power, but thank God, that was never His intention. God knows we can't even pray to Him without His help. The disciples asked to be taught to pray. I think it's time that we do the same. There is no better time to start than now, and there is no better way to begin learning than by asking the Teacher to help.

> If my people, who are called by my name humble themselves, and pray and seek my face and turn from their wicked ways, then I will hear from heaven and will forgive their sin and heal their land. (2 Chronicles 7:14 ESV)

CHAPTER 9

NEVER PRAY FOR PATIENCE

I'm very aware that this statement is typically made in a joking manner. The humor in it is not lost on me. This phrase has been spoken by people in every generation, new Christians and seasoned ones alike. The reasoning behind the joke is usually as follows: "I prayed for patience, and instead of giving me patience, God gave me opportunities to be patient." It isn't fun to practice patience. Being patient is not usually an enjoyable process because we don't enjoy waiting, and we definitely do not enjoy suffering while we wait.

I understand the sentiment. The problem here is that I've noticed a trend in newer or less seasoned believers who truly believe that we are instructed by God not to pray for patience because they have heard it stated so often. This idea has instilled a belief that patience is a good thing, but it's too dangerous to pray for. It creates a fear of praying for what we need in case God decides to use that prayer to make us sorry that we asked for it. That is not the character of God. He does not use your prayers as ammunition against you.

I remember in elementary and even high school that it was common practice to avoid eye contact with the teacher, especially when the teacher was calling on students to answer questions about the material being covered in the class. The very second you made eye contact, you could rest assured that you would be the next person called on. It seems that this is how we've started to view praying for patience. We avoid it altogether in hopes that less will be required of us.

God is not waiting on you to address a subject to put you on the spot. As we have learned through this study on the Word, God wants us to follow His ways, and He wants to help us, strengthen us, and sustain us as we are sanctified. God will never punish you for seeking to be more like Him. Trials will be a part of that sanctification often, not because God is waiting on the chance to dump them on you but because trials produce endurance and endurance produces strength.

First Peter 4:12 says, "Dear friends, don't be surprised when the fiery ordeal comes among you to test you as if something unusual were happening to you." Fiery ordeals, trials, tests, grievances, and annoyances will come among you because we are flesh living in a fallen creation that is infected with sin. When we recognize that suffering is a part of life instead of an attack or form of retaliation from God, we will see that we truly have a need for supernatural patience to endure.

Earlier in 1 Peter 1:6–7, it says, "You rejoice in this, even though now for a short time, if necessary, you suffer grief in various trials so that the proven character of your faith—more valuable than gold which, though perishable, is refined by fire—may result in praise, glory, and honor at the revelation of Jesus Christ." Those trials that we face have purpose when we are in Jesus. The character of our faith is revealed, refined, and strengthened through trials.

In Matthew chapter 7, Jesus addresses this idea that asking God for something we need will put us in the place to receive something bad from Him instead. He says in verse 7, "Ask, and it will be given to you. Seek, and you will find. Knock, and the door will be opened to you." Then later in verses 9–11, He says, "Who among you, if his son asks for bread, will give him a stone? Or if he asks for a fish, will give him a snake? If you then, who are evil, know how to give good gifts to your children, how much more will your Father in heaven give good things to those who ask him."

God is our Father. He loves us as His children and heirs with Jesus as we learn in Romans 8:17. Parents will allow their children to walk through challenges when necessary to learn an important lesson. However, a loving, just, and kind parent will never multiply troubles for their children for personal entertainment. You can rest assured that whatever trial you are walking through, God sees it and allowed it for a specific purpose. Suffering is never in vain.

> But the fruit of the Spirit is love, joy, peace, patience, kindness, goodness, faithfulness, gentleness, and self-control. (Galatians 5:22–23 CSB)

The fruit of the Spirit has been a key scripture reference point in many of the chapters we have walked through together. Here, in the discussion of patience, we must visit it once again. The fruit of the Spirit is a singular fruit with nine virtues. Patience is one of these virtues. Instructing people not to pray for an attribute that is part of the Spirit of God creates a false view of the Holy Spirit as a villain. And because we have established that God cannot be separated from His Spirit, it creates a negative view of an attribute of God as well. The Holy Spirit is a part of God, so any characteristic of the Holy Spirit is also a characteristic of God.

If that feels like too much of a stretch to you, here is further evidence. In 1 Corinthians chapter 13, as Paul lays out the characteristics of true love, he says in verse 4 that love is patient. Going further, in verse 7 he states that love endures all things. In 1 John chapter 4, it is repeated that God *is* love. God takes love as a quality of His nature. God is love, and true love is patient, so we know for certain that patience is a quality of our God. Redeemed followers of Jesus are carriers of the Holy Spirit, and we know that God helps us to love like Him, so patience should also be one of our attributes.

In case you're still not sold on the patience of God, here is one more verse that lays it out very plainly. Second Peter 3:9 says, "The Lord does not delay his promise, as some understand delay, but is patient with you, not wanting any to perish but all to come to repentance." His patient nature is displayed by the way He delays His wrath and offers salvation to all. How could it ever be wrong to pray for a quality that makes us more like God?

In fact, we know from our study on discipleship that disciples are trained to be like their teacher. First John 2:6 tells us that if we abide in Him, we should walk in the manner in which He walked. John is referring to Jesus here. Jesus is one part of the Holy Trinity, so we know that He is not separate from God or the Holy Spirit either. The manner in which Jesus walked absolutely portrayed patience because He carries the attributes of God and the Spirit!

Looking deeper into prayer in the previous chapter, we learned that it is important to pray in accordance with the will of God. In Ephesians 4:22–24, Paul encourages believers to take off their old self that is tainted by their former ways and put on the new self that is created according to God's likeness. It is absolutely within the will of God for us to pray for God to help us put on the new self that looks like Him. How else will we begin to look more like Him if we don't ask for His help in doing so? Jesus said if we ask, it will be given.

Nowhere in the Bible will you find a verse that says praying for patience is not recommended or that it will bring you trials or obstacles, but remember from our very first chapter, we will face hardships and trials while in the world because we abide in God. The opportunity to be patient will come whether you pray for patience or not. What a comfort to know that God can provide every ounce of patience we need when those trying opportunities do come. That knowledge alone shifts the theme of this chapter from avoiding praying for patience to relying on and praying for the Lord to help you walk in His power and love, with patience being a part of that.

> Therefore, as God's chosen ones, holy and dearly loved, put on compassion, kindness, humility, gentleness, and patience, bearing with one another and forgiving one another if anyone has a grievance against another. Just as the Lord has forgiven you, so you are also to forgive. (Colossians 3:12–13 CSB)

I have driven this statement into the ground, but I'm repeating it again because it is so important to grasp. God will not instruct us to do something that He cannot or will not empower us to do. Here in Colossians, we are instructed to put on patience. You will only be able to put on patience through the power of the Holy Spirit working within you. Putting on patience has a lot less to do with what is going on around you than it does with He who is in you.

Putting on patience means being patient with family and friends during disagreements. It means being patient with the server who brought food to the table that arrived after you and still hasn't taken your drink order. It means controlling your emotions and dealing gracefully with the temper tantrum your toddler is throwing. Another word that can be used when talking about patience is long-suffering. Enduring a long struggle is an example of patience.

Situations like these are simply a part of life, not a retaliation from God because you prayed for His patience. The key thing that I want to reiterate here circles back to our first chapter. God's strength will sustain you in your weaknesses and will be displayed in those same weaknesses. You don't have the power to suffer well on your own. You don't have the ability to respond gracefully. You don't have the strength to remain patient. But you are not alone if you are in Christ. You are not reliant on your own strength anymore.

> Even youths shall faint and be weary, and young men shall fall exhausted; but those who wait on the Lord shall renew their strength; they shall mount up with wings like eagles; they shall run and not be weary; they shall walk and not grow faint. (Isaiah 40:30-31 ESV)

Sometimes, putting on patience will even require you to be patient with and wait on God. His timing is vastly different from our own. Second Peter 3:8 says that to God a day is like a thousand years, and a thousand years is like a day. God is outside of time because He created time. While this can seem overwhelming for our human minds to process, it really is encouraging for us. God sees all of time, and we know His ways and plans are good. He knows the perfect time for everything.

It's easy to become frustrated with God when things we pray for don't happen in the time line we expected. We've gotten extremely reliant on the fast-paced culture of today that promises instant results. God has the wisdom and foresight to know when instant results to a prayer we prayed could be the difference between life and death.

In Daniel chapter 10, Daniel had received a message from God about a great conflict through a vision. He wanted to understand the vision fully, and so for three weeks or twenty-one days, he fasted and prayed. After the three weeks were up, Daniel had another vision, and in it, the messenger tells him in verse 12, "For from the first day that you purposed to understand and to humble yourself before your God, your prayers were heard. I have come because of your prayers. But the prince of the kingdom of Persia opposed me for twenty-one days."

There is debate about whether Daniel was speaking to an angel or if this was Jesus speaking to him because of the similarities in John's description of Jesus in Revelation chapter 1. However, most agree that the prince of the kingdom of Persia refers to Satan. This account shows that our prayers are heard but that there are happenings in the spiritual realm that we have no knowledge of. A delayed answer from God is always for a specific reason. I love the way Daniel waited patiently and even committed himself to fasting during his wait. He was confident that God would help him understand the message at the right time.

Over and over throughout Scripture, we find the command to wait on the Lord. But look what happens in our verses from Isaiah when we do wait on the Lord. The Word says that we will renew our strength! I love the way David talks about waiting on the Lord through prayer in Psalm chapter 5. In verse 3, he says, "In the morning, Lord, you hear my voice; in the morning I plead my case to you and watch expectantly." David lays before God the concerns tugging at his heart and then watches expectantly. He never put a time line on the watching-expectedly portion. He was confident that God would move. And he was confident God would move in the way He knew was good and perfectly timed. Praying for patience could actually be a gift during your wait!

> Let us not get tired of doing good, for we
> will reap at the proper time if we don't give up.
> (Galatians 6:9)

If you've ever been taken advantage of for being kind or doing a good thing for another person, you will understand the patience required in continuing to do good rather than giving up. Patience is a necessity in the life of a follower of Jesus. There is no way around it. This verse from Galatians is just one example of biblical instruction that requires patience to accomplish what the Lord calls for. I wanted to list a few examples of instructions we receive throughout the Word that require patience for you to study through on your own.

- Ephesians 4:1–3
- Psalm 37:7–8
- Ecclesiastes 7:8–9
- James 1:19–20
- James 1:26
- James 5:7–8
- Romans 15:4–6
- Romans 8:24–25

These are just a few of the verses I could list. What I really hope you see is that we need the patience of God to run the race set before us as followers of Jesus. We desperately need God to equip us with the ability to remain faithful through trials and to practice long-suffering when it is required. James says in verse 2 of chapter 4, "You do not have because you do not ask." Is it possible that you do not have patience because you are refusing to or are afraid to ask God for it?

Something really incredible to me about praying for patience or, honestly, just praying in general is that it doesn't have to be a big theatrical declaration. When you feel that you are losing control of your emotions, all it takes is a quick, silent prayer. You don't have to drop to your knees at the customer service desk and loudly ask God for the patience to continue the termination of your cell phone service. A simple, internal prayer of "Lord, give me patience" is enough.

It isn't necessary that you wait for a time of peace in your life to ask for more patience. God is ever-present. In the middle of a great time of need is the perfect time to call on Him for strength. There would be no need for God to be with us always if the times we could call out to Him were limited. He truly cares for you. He really does want to strengthen you as you face weaknesses.

So pray for patience, but don't stop there! Pray for love and joy. Pray for peace. Pray to have the qualities of goodness, kindness, faithfulness, and gentleness. Ask God to strengthen your self-control (which, ironically enough, will require patience as well). Even more than that, pray that God would increase your sensitivity to the Holy Spirit when He is prompting you to act with these qualities rather than selfish ones. The Holy Spirit is the good gift to us as followers of Jesus.

CHAPTER 10

I Don't Have to Attend Church to Be Saved

Church can be a touchy subject. You'll find believers who are passionate advocates for meeting together with a church body and ones who are passionately against it. Some truly believe that it is completely unnecessary. After the whirlwind that was 2020, I'm afraid this sentiment is even more widely believed. Worldwide, churches shut their doors and congregational meetings stopped. Online streaming services were an incredible gift during this time, yet virtual attendance dropped dramatically as the pandemic wore on as well.

What was a priority for a lot of people became optional and then became unimportant. Eventually, as meeting together was reinstated, many people never returned. Isolation is one of Satan's biggest advantages. He used this time of forced isolation to increase the volume of many of his lies, but especially the lie that meeting together is unnecessary. Looking at the state of the world today, I truly believe it proves that isolation is a breeding ground for sin and evil as well.

Aside from viewing church as unimportant, another major reason I hear this argument that attending church is not a salvation requirement usually stems from negative experiences with church or church people in the past. This is often referred to as "church hurt." People hurt people. Sometimes hurt is intentional; many times, it is not. Yet the truth of the matter is that you will never encounter perfect people in this world who say and do the right thing all the time.

I wish I could say that this applies everywhere except inside a church, but you and I both know that church people still mess up and sin.

Church hurt is very real and is, unfortunately, the reason that so many professing believers are not members of a local church body. The natural response to experiencing pain is to remove yourself from the source of the pain. This hurt has spilled over generationally in many families as well resulting in a cycle of people who choose to remove themselves from anything resembling organized religion at all. Where people are involved, things get messy.

Church attendance is not what saves you. Receiving the salvation of Jesus can happen anywhere and at any time. Being in a church building when you repent and choose to follow Jesus does not make you anymore saved or holy than repenting and choosing Jesus in your car. Salvation doesn't come from any pastor or teacher. Salvation only comes from Jesus and His blood. Keep in mind, that also means that not every person you encounter within a church body truly knows Jesus. The hurt you've experienced may have very well been at the hands of one of those people. Weekly church attendance no more makes you a Christian than sitting on a grocery store shelf makes you a loaf of bread.

Chances are, even in your immediate circle, you will find many opinions on church. Our preferences have a way of dictating what we believe as truth. But I hope that the one thing you've learned through the words on the previous pages of this book is that we must go to the true source to get the true answer. So, what does the Bible say about meeting together with other believers?

> Let us hold on to the confession of our hope without wavering, since he who promised is faithful. And let us watch out for one another to provoke love and good works, not neglecting to gather together, as some are in the habit of doing, but encouraging each other, and all the more as you see the day approaching. (Hebrews 10:23–25 CSB)

First things first, what is the approaching day that is referred to here? If we look back to verses 12–13, we see a description of Jesus that says, "But this man, after offering one sacrifice for sins forever, sat down at the right hand of God. He is now waiting until his enemies are made his footstool." The approaching day is the day that God's wrath is poured out on His enemies. This happens at the end of this age. This sentence is drawing our attention to the coming of Christ, which ushers in the destruction of this world and its systems and the revealing of the eternal reign of Jesus.

I have briefly mentioned this in pages prior, but prophecy points to the signs of the times, and it is very clear that this day is rapidly approaching. Here we find that rather than meet together less, we are instructed to meet together *all the more* as we see the day of Christ draw near. Remember that every word recorded in our Bibles was written by man through inspiration from God. When God instructed this phrase to be written, He already knew that a pandemic was coming in the year 2020. He already foresaw that church doors would be closed. Yet He still gave the instruction to meet together even more.

It is chilling to read these verses penned so long ago and see such an accurate description of the culture of today. There is absolutely a habit of neglecting to meet together. Even more so now than ever before. We cannot do as we are instructed and watch out for each other from a computer screen. Watching a church meet together online is essentially the same as watching a television show. You don't become a part of the cast or crew of a show by sitting on your couch, watching what they produce. God values true relationship, and the way He instituted the Church proves that.

God can absolutely move through an online recording of a message. You aren't doing wrong by watching or listening to videos of sermons to learn, provided that they line up with the Word of God. The problem comes when we accept virtual meetings alone as a substitute for the community that God is so clearly calling us to. Remember Jesus said in Matthew 18:20 that where two or more gather in His name, He is there among them! There is no substitute for your private time with God, but please understand that something incredible happens when the people of God come together in His name.

There are a few verses in Genesis that give such a beautiful illustration of this. In chapter 29, Jacob is on a journey to find a wife for himself when he sees a field with a well. Around the well, three flocks of sheep were gathered because this is where the shepherds of the land watered their flocks. Verse 3 says, "The shepherds would roll the stone from the opening of the well and water the sheep when all the flocks were gathered there." Until the flocks were gathered, the well remained closed off.

Jesus said that He is the source of living water in John chapter 4. How fitting that to access this well of water, the shepherds had to roll a stone away from the opening. The sheep probably had sips of water from other sources as they journeyed, and we know they would graze in different areas, which would hydrate them some as well. However, when they were unified together at the well, they drank deeply from the water offered. Meeting together in church can't be your only time spent in communion with God, but there is no denying that there is a special outpouring within the body of Christ meeting in unity.

In the book of Psalms, you will find several chapters that are labeled as a "song of ascents." These were literal songs or hymns that the people would sing as they traveled to Jerusalem to worship at the temple. In Psalm 122, David begins these songs by saying, "I rejoiced with those who said to me, 'Let us go to the house of the Lord." Later he described the tribes of the Lord going up to give thanks to the Lord and specified that it was an ordinance for Israel to gather together to worship in Jerusalem. The gathering together of God's people was commanded even in the Old Testament times before Jesus came.

Because our God dwells within His people now rather than in a temple, the way we gather together as individual churches looks much different. We don't have to travel to Jerusalem at certain times of the year to worship God together. We can do that in our homes, church buildings, and even as we gather around a table to share a meal. Just because gathering together doesn't involve a temple anymore doesn't make it any less vital to the life of a follower of Jesus.

In 1 Corinthians chapters 13 and 14, while Paul speaks about spiritual gifts and the way they should be handled in the churches, in verse 26 of chapter 14, he begins an instruction about these gifts with these words: "Whenever you come together..." Coming together was a sure thing. There was no question about if it were to happen in his statement. We are called to gather together as the body of Christ.

In John chapter 10, Jesus describes Himself as the Good Shepherd, and we who follow Him as the sheep of His flock. In verse 16, He says, "But I have other sheep that are not from this sheep pen; I must bring them also, and they will listen to my voice. Then there will be one flock, one shepherd." Jesus didn't choose sheep for this example randomly. My family has recently begun raising sheep, and one of the things I love the most about them is watching how tightly knit the flock is. They generally travel together. You will very rarely find one that wanders a great distance from the rest of the herd. All the new lambs group together to play and learn regardless of which ewe birthed them.

They will separate into smaller groups; some will walk away for a spell alone. The new mothers will sometimes fall back in distance while nursing their lambs, and the older rams get caught up disciplining the young rams, but even as they take time away, they are still mostly in a unit. They always meet back together, especially when food is offered. When my husband or father-in-law come to the barn and call, "Here, babies!" they immediately come running expectantly, knowing that an abundance of nutrients is waiting. Do you see the beautiful symbolism in this? Jesus says when we gather together in His name, He is there. All we have to do is listen to the call and show up.

Jesus prayed before He went to the cross that we would be one, just as He and the Father are one. He has an abundance to offer us when we gather. Yes, meeting together can get messy, and sometimes there is drama involved, but that is just part of spending time around other people in any setting. You can't escape those things in your family, workplace, or even a shopping trip to Walmart for groceries. You still spend time with your family because you live in the same home. You still go to work because the paycheck is necessary to sustain your lifestyle. You continue to shop at Walmart or other stores because you have a need for the things they have for sale. The benefit outweighs the hardship.

> He exercised this power in Christ by raising him from the dead and seating him at his right hand in the heavens—far above every ruler and authority, power and dominion, and every title given, not only in this age but also in the one to come. And he subjected everything under his feet and appointed him as head over everything for the church, which is his body, the fullness of the one who fills all things in every way. (Ephesians 1:20–23)

When we speak about church, the meaning is sometimes misconstrued, especially in current times. Here in Ephesians chapter 1, we get the simplest definition. The church is the body of Christ. Christ is the head of the global church, and the church is the fullness of the One who fills it. By repenting of sin and receiving the redemption, forgiveness, and salvation of Jesus, you become a part of the church. The Greek word used for church in this aspect is *ecclesia,* which loosely defined means "the called out gathering."

The body of Christ is called to meet together, and those individual meetings are what we call "church." Christ is not coming back for His brides, plural; He is coming back for His singular bride. Unity has always been the design of the bride. When we choose to exist outside of that unity, we are putting ourselves outside of the will of God and the original design of God.

In all of this, you could still say that our beginning quote has not been proven wrong. Going to church isn't required for you to receive salvation. The Bible never says that to be saved, you must regularly attend church. However, it does say that disciples of Jesus abide by the Word of God. Remember, Jesus said in John 8:31, "If you continue in my word, you really are my disciples." We have just seen proof the Word we are called to abide in and continue in tells us to meet together.

Church is not a requirement of salvation, but surrendering to the will of the Father is. The will of God is revealed to us in His Word. Part of His will is the gathering together of His people. If we claim Jesus as Savior, we must submit to Him as Lord. Submitting to Him as Lord means we put priority on the things He emphasizes rather than our own preferences. In Matthew 16:24, Jesus says, "If anyone wants to follow after me, let him deny himself, take up his cross, and follow me."

Reading the Bible is not required to be saved. Neither is being baptized, praying, loving others, or making disciples. However, if we leave out the things that should happen after salvation, we are teaching a false gospel. Jesus never asked us to pray a prayer for forgiveness and then live in the way we saw fit. Jesus said that to truly follow Him, we have to deny ourselves. None of these works will save you, but being saved by Jesus will lead us to obedience in the things He calls for.

I love the account of Philip and the Ethiopian official found in Acts 8:26–40. God told Philip to get up and go to a specific road that traveled from Jerusalem to Gaza. Once there, he overheard this official reading aloud from the book of Isaiah as he traveled in his chariot. The Holy Spirit instructed Philip to join the man's chariot, and as he does this, he asks the man in verse 30, "Do you understand what you're reading?" The Ethiopian official responds, "How can I unless someone guides me?"

This interaction opened the door for Philip to explain the Scriptures and tell this man the good news of Jesus. As the chariot travels, they come to an area that has water of some sort. The official says to Philip in verse 36, "Look, there's water. What would keep me from being baptized?" Immediately after hearing the truth of Jesus and receiving Him as Lord, this man responded in obedience and was baptized. He didn't view a command of the Lord as optional after he met Jesus as Savior. He recognized that Jesus as His Lord required obedience.

Jesus didn't come to be a supplement to your life. He didn't come to provide you with a ticket to heaven. He came to take the punishment for sin that would kill your soul. He came to shed the blood required to pay the debt you owed. He came to bridge the gap between you and God that was created by sin. When He lays out these requirements in the Word, it is for the good of those He calls.

As we learned in Romans 8:28, God works all things for the good. Because of this knowledge, we can rest assured that the guidelines He puts in place are for our good as well. My understanding of why God chooses to do things a certain way is not necessary, but my obedience is. If I can trust that Jesus coming to die for my sin was a beneficial thing for me, I can also trust that being a part of a church that honors God is beneficial too. In fact, we can even find scripture that gives us reasons for why it is a good thing for us.

First Corinthians 14:26 tells us that as we meet together, the church is built up. Meeting together will draw in unbelievers who, because of the unity, love, and display of the gospel of Christ, can come to the saving knowledge of Christ. In Ecclesiastes 4:9–10, it says, "Two are better than one because they have a good reward for their efforts. For if either falls, his companion can lift him up; but pity the one who falls without another to lift him up." We also build each other up! We are meant to help bear each other's burdens.

We've already covered Proverbs 27:17 that tells us we can sharpen each other as iron sharpens iron. Proverbs 13:20 says that walking with wise people begins to make us wise as well. Wisdom comes from God, so walking with people who are grounded in the Word and grounded in their relationship with Jesus is important here. On the flip side, 1 Corinthians 15:33 warns that bad company will ruin good morals. While we know that not every person you meet in a church will be wisely walking with the Lord or living out good morals, many are. There are fruitful relationships that can be built through your local church.

In our featured scripture of Hebrews 10:23–25, the writer urges us to stir one another up to love and do good works before encouraging us not to neglect meeting together. As we meet together, we can encourage each other in the way we love others. We can also help build the faith of each other through our testimonies. We discussed prophecy earlier where Paul says in 1 Corinthians 14 that it will build up the church. Remember that prophecy is a message from God. In Revelation 19:10, we learn that the spirit of prophecy is the testimony of Jesus. As we use the gift of prophecy or speaking the Word of God, we testify about Jesus and His redemption. Our testimonies, intertwined with the way Jesus has marked and saved us, build the faith of those around us!

One of my favorite examples of the power of testimony is found in John chapter 4. Jesus sat down at a well in Samaria, tired and thirsty from traveling. A woman was there alone at the well in the hottest part of the day. Jesus asked this woman for a drink of water. She was blown away that a Jewish man was speaking to her because Samaritans and Jews didn't mix. Besides that, she had been in and out of marriages and was currently living with a man she was not married to.

Coming to the well in the hottest part of the day was to avoid the shame of seeing other women at the well at cooler times. She was ashamed of her reputation. Jesus eventually told her that He knew all the shameful things in her past and revealed to her that He is in fact the Messiah. This woman immediately left the jar of water she had brought to the well and in verse 29 runs into the town saying, "Come, see a man who told me everything I ever did. Could this be the Messiah?"

Later in verse 39, the Bible tells us that many people believed in Jesus as the Messiah because of what this woman said. They came to meet Jesus and invited Him to stay with them, and He did stay for two days. In verse 42, after spending time with Jesus, we see where people of the town told this woman, "We no longer believe because of what you said, since we have heard for ourselves and know that this really is the Savior of the world." The testimony of this woman opened the door for the people in Samaria to truly encounter Jesus and acknowledge Him as Messiah.

This is a very abridged version of an incredible account, so please take the time to read the full story in John chapter 4! Jesus does the transformation, but we get to be a part of spreading the message about who He is. If this woman's testimony alone was enough to bring people to seek Jesus further, can you imagine the power that comes from a gathering of people declaring the greatness of God? Not just to the outside world or unbelievers but even to the believers in attendance as well!

Faith comes from hearing the message of Jesus as Romans 10:17 tells us. If you struggle in the category of faith, one of the most beneficial things you can do for yourself is to get into a group of people who are discussing the Word of God and sharing testimony of the power of God. So much of the Bible is account after account of God and His power. The Israelites recount their history with God so often in the Old Testament for this very reason. It was so important to them that future generations had access to the wonderful, mighty acts of God that happened in the past so that their faith was built in Him as well.

Meeting together also gives us the benefit of accountability. While being held accountable can be a tough pill to swallow, it truly is necessary. James 5:16 says, "Therefore, confess your sins to one another and pray for one another, so that you may be healed. The prayer of a righteous person is very powerful in its effect." For those of you whom this verse just terrified, this does not mean you will be required to tell all your past sins when you become a part of a church body. No one is going to ask for a list of your wrongdoings before allowing you to enter their church. If they do, run!

Confessing our sins to one another can be as simple as confiding in a trusted friend or group of friends about an area you are struggling through in your walk with Christ. Keep in mind that as we confess our sin, the appropriate biblical response of the hearer is prayer. This should not become an opportunity to gossip or a chance to store up information to use against that person later. The Bible is clear about our need for accountability, but it is also extremely clear about our conduct and intentions in carrying it out.

Traveling further in James chapter 5, in verse 19, it says, "My brothers and sisters, if any among you strays from the truth, and someone turns him back, let that person know that whoever turns a sinner from the error of his way will save his soul from death and cover a multitude of sins." This verse sounds a great deal like what we learned earlier about discipleship. As we disciple others through truth, we must also do it with love and gentleness as we see in Galatians 6:1. Even though being corrected can be painful, it is truly a gift to have friends who care for your spiritual health enough to lovingly offer you the truth of God's Word.

Looking back on the topic of church hurt, I feel it is important to reiterate that if you claim to be a follower of Jesus, being held accountable for your actions is completely biblical. If you have been corrected and held accountable in a church in a way that honors the Word of God, you have not been hurt by the church, you have been hurt by your sin. If someone loves you enough to come to you with biblical correction, that is a gift from God, not a church hurt. If the correction was unbiblical or fueled by anything other than love, that is a completely different story. However, we cannot villainize godly correction.

> So then you are no longer foreigners and strangers, but fellow citizens with the saints, and members of God's household, built on the foundation of the apostles and prophets, with Christ Jesus himself as the cornerstone. In him the whole building, being put together, grows into a holy temple in the Lord. In him you are also being built together for God's dwelling in the Spirit. (Ephesians 2:19–22)

Once we were foreigners and strangers, but through Jesus Christ, we are now a part of a family. Christ is the cornerstone, and we are built together in Him. Unity in His bride was the plan from the beginning. God values people, and He values relationship. He called us into unity because it is good. He called us to meet together because it's just another way that He sanctifies and sustains us. Don't miss this good plan of God's because of fear or dislike.

If the churches you have tried weren't the right fit, keep trying. Here in America, there is no shortage of churches. You probably drive past several on your daily commute. The most important thing to look for when searching for a home church is one that teaches and abides by the Word of God. The church must be founded on the cornerstone that is Jesus, and any foundation that contradicts the Word is not one that is reliant on Jesus.

Small groups are excellent ways to meet together on a smaller scale as well. If you're already plugged into a church body, check into what your church offers for smaller gatherings. If nothing is offered, talk with leadership about providing those opportunities. Smaller groups can sometimes lessen the anxiety that can come with meeting or getting to know new people. As with anything, begin with prayer. Ask God to show you where to go. Ask Him to help you as you walk in obedience to His Word. He won't give you instructions and then leave you to struggle through on your own!

IMPORTANT FINAL
THOUGHTS

Don't Skip This Chapter

Writing this book was a daunting task. Not because of the work so much as the internal struggle that came along with it. I felt the weight of the burden in a way that I can't truly put into words. I debated with myself about changing the entire thing to make it more palatable. I worried that what I was writing was too legalistic and divisive. My fear was that my writing would seem judgmental or that people would decide my goal was to make them feel negatively about believing or repeating any of the addressed phrases. Even worse, I feared that I wouldn't do God's grace the justice that it deserves, leaving readers feeling defeated and unable to adhere to His standards.

Most of these covered phrases have exited my mouth in the past. I believed a vast number of them over my lifetime. My decision to write this book came from a process of the Lord unraveling the threads of my own tradition that I had attempted to weave into the tapestry of His truth. He has so lovingly walked with me through this disentangling. I know that my remaining years on earth will be filled with more of this journey because God continues to have more to teach me.

When I mentioned in the introductory chapter that God has grace for the process of growth, I meant it. I have been a recipient of that grace. I can truly attest to it because I have lived in it. I shudder remembering things I have said in the past with the best intentions that were flat-out wrong. But, as a dear friend reminded me, I can never surprise or catch God off guard. Even the worst parts of my story were already anticipated by Him. He is so very patient with us in the process.

The reason I wanted to include this final chapter with a much more personal tone is because I so strongly believe that there is power in testimony. There is nothing about me that is deserving of this grace or wisdom that God is sharing with me. I was a decent student in school, average in most regards. I am now a stay-at-home wife and mom to one sweet girl and, at the time this chapter is being written, a baby boy on the way. There is nothing spectacular about me in any way. But I met Jesus in His Word, and He changed my life.

I met the real Jesus through the inspired, living, eternal Word of God. Not the American Jesus we see on posters and T-shirts. Not the culturally accepted Jesus who simply wants everyone to coexist in love and harmony while finding their own version of truth. I met the Father who loved me so much He was willing to sacrifice His only Son to bring me into His family. I met the Holy Spirit who teaches me, corrects me, refines me, and comforts me daily. I encountered the Lord who is part of His Word. I cannot remain the same, and I cannot silently sit with the things I've learned.

Psalm 50 has been a huge catalyst in this season for me. In verse 16, it says, "But God says to the wicked: 'What right do you have to recite my statutes and to take my covenant on your lips? You hate instruction and fling my words behind you.'" This verse describes my actions for so many years. For the majority of my new life in Christ, I flung His Words behind me. I claimed Jesus, yet I had no idea of the instruction that He had for me in His Word. It took me fifteen years to realize that I needed to read every syllable contained in my Bible because the God I claimed to love had inspired every single one.

I may not have outwardly hated His instruction, but I ignored it, which is close to the same. I did not know what God instructed or asked of me, because I didn't study His Word. I did not know His story and the way His grace is woven in from beginning to end. I didn't truly know who God was, because I didn't know Him through His Word. I didn't trust the Holy Spirit enough to teach me the things I didn't understand. In fact, I didn't even know that was one of His responsibilities.

Later, in verse 21 of Psalm 50, God says, "You have done these things, and I kept silent; you thought I was just like you." My heart aches when I read this verse. I am currently typing this sentence with tears falling down my cheeks because of how closely my past resembles this statement. I did think God was just like me. I thought I had all the knowledge of Him I needed because I was saved. I put my attributes onto the God of the universe. I kept my traditions and believed they belonged to Him. I took my regular Sunday seat, posted my encouraging social media statuses, and lived my life with little alteration to my own behavior or priorities.

I lived a very selfish, preference-driven life believing that God was just like my preferences. God is not like me. He is holy. He is just. He is gracious. He is merciful. His love is faithful. His compassion is abundant. His ways are good. His instruction is good. When He gives instruction or sets boundaries, it is never without purpose. When He gives specifics on what He requires to follow Him, He is serious.

I hope that my words accurately portray the importance of devotion to His ways and His Word, but I hope they also accurately describe the way that He helps us do the things He requires. Pleasing God is not attainable without the help of God. The beautiful thing about Him is that He knows this and offers everything we need. Please hear my heart's cry when I tell you that He really will do the things He promises. My life is a testament to that. The composition of this book is a giant testament to His faithfulness.

But, as I've mentioned many times now, order matters in the kingdom of God. I would be doing a disservice to you if I did not include this next part. You cannot access the strength of God without first repenting of your sin, asking for the forgiveness of that sin, confessing Jesus Christ as Lord, and submitting to Him as Lord. You cannot follow Jesus without first truly receiving the salvation of Jesus.

In the depths of my being, I believe that there are people who right now believe that they are saved because they repeated a prayer to keep them from hell. The Bible never instructs us to repeat a certain prayer to be saved. Prayer alone is not what saves you. Serving at your church, being kind to others, and living a "good" life is not what saves you. Repeatedly, all throughout the Scriptures, we see it stated that salvation is through faith alone and by grace alone. Ephesians 2:8–9 tells us that salvation is not a result of works so that no one can boast.

You cannot be saved without repentance and dying to self. This message is difficult to hear. That's why Jesus says in Matthew 7:13–14 that few find the road to eternal life because it is narrow. Dying to self is not our first choice, especially in a culture that promotes finding your own truth and indulging every whim and desire. Many people believe this teaching is works-based or legalistic, but I cannot alter or soften what Jesus said. Jesus cannot resurrect something that has not yet died. This is the way to eternal life.

Before you close this book and continue on with whatever tasks await you next, do as 2 Corinthians 13:5 says and examine yourself to see if you are truly in the faith. Evaluate the fruit in your life as we discussed. The fruit of the Spirit was not recorded only for us to evaluate the lives of others, but our own lives first. None of the words on the previous pages matter until you have solidified your faith and salvation in Jesus. Until you are given new life by Jesus the Savior, the things I've written are just a tangle of rules and regulations. Jesus is the difference maker.

You can possess all the biblical knowledge in the world, but if you miss Jesus, you have missed it all. In John chapter 3, you can read the conversation Jesus has with a Pharisee named Nicodemus. Being a Pharisee, Nicodemus had extensive knowledge of the Word. He came to Jesus at night—probably hoping not to have his reputation marred by being seen with Jesus—attempting to make sense of this man who was performing signs and miracles and fulfilling prophecy. Jesus tells Nicodemus that to see the kingdom of God, he must be born again. In this conversation with Nicodemus, we find the very well-known scripture in verse 16, "For God loved the world in this way: He gave his one and only Son, so that everyone who believes in him will not perish but have eternal life."

To have eternal life, we must believe in Jesus as the Son of God and be born again. We are born in the flesh and into sin as we enter this world as a newborn baby. Being born again requires being born of the Spirit. Later, Jesus says that anyone who lives by the truth comes to the light so that his works can be shown to be accomplished by God. We do not work to earn salvation, but from salvation comes the works of new life in Christ.

The account of Nicodemus's conversation with Jesus ends here. Many of the Pharisees did not accept Jesus as the Messiah. In fact, the Pharisees were a major part in having Jesus crucified. But if we travel ahead to John 19:38–42, we learn that Nicodemus may not have been one of the Pharisees who denied Jesus. After Jesus died on the cross, a man named Joseph of Arimathea came to remove Jesus's body and take Him to the tomb He would be buried in. In verse 39, we learn that Nicodemus also came and brought with him myrrh and aloes with which to anoint Jesus's body for burial.

This man who came to Jesus in secret was now displaying what appears to be devotion to Him in public. His actions seem to show that Nicodemus died to his old self and was born again into the new life of truly following Jesus. This is what it means to choose Jesus. Second Peter 3:9 specifies that the Lord desires all to come to repentance. Repentance is turning away from things that dishonor God and turning toward Him instead.

If you can move on from here, certain of your security in Jesus, if you still have questions about the topics you've read here, or if you are even questioning this whole faith thing in general, I have one more challenge for you. In Acts 17:10–15, Paul and Silas are sent to minister in a place called Berea. When they arrive in Berea, they go immediately to the Jewish synagogue. The account says in verse 11, "The people here were of more noble character than those in Thessalonica, since they received the word with eagerness and examined the scriptures daily to see if these things were so." Because of their eagerness in searching the Scripture for themselves, the Bible tells us that many of them believed.

Receive the words I've written to you with eagerness, but please do not stop there. Do as these Bereans did and search the Scriptures for yourself to see if what I have written is true. I implore you to do so. The Word says that if we seek God, we will find Him. I am more than confident that you will meet the same Jesus I did. I am not the final authority on anything, but the One who is can be found within His Word through the help of His Holy Spirit.

Disciples live in the Word of God, and disciples begin to look like their teacher. In John chapter 1, Jesus is described as the Word made flesh. Jesus walking on earth was the physical embodiment of this Word. He fulfilled the laws and prophecies. He confirmed every scripture. The Word was God, was with God, and was made flesh in the coming of our Messiah, Yeshua. You cannot look like Jesus without this Word. It is not possible. Jesus is the Word made flesh. You cannot be a disciple without looking like the Word of God.

The Word calls for obedience which also calls for action. You are not saved by your works, but following Jesus will come with being obedient to work for the Lord in the way the Bible lays out. There is no way to separate the two. If you are seeing no works in your faith, you must evaluate that faith. Devotion to Jesus is shown by living out the Word.

Do not start this journey without first going to the Lord in prayer. Ask Him to give you hunger for the Word. He keeps you fed, but even in that filling, He can keep you hungry for more of Him. Ask God to send His Holy Spirit to you in a greater measure. Ask Him for every good gift of the Spirit that He has planned for you. Ask for wisdom and understanding as you seek Him. God will not deny a heart that desires to know Him.

Ask Him to reveal any tradition or ideal you hold that is not from Him. Ask Him for grace in the time of growth. He will provide. If you need a boost of faith, ask Him. God wants a relationship with you. He wants to reveal Himself to you. His invitation to seek Him is still open.

Jesus told him, "I am the way, the truth, and the life. No one comes to the Father except through me. If you know me, you will also know my Father." (John 14:6–7 CSB)

ABOUT THE AUTHOR

Savannah Sibert is a wife and mother who has loved writing and songwriting from a young age. She believes that God has given her these interests to exalt His name. She is passionate about the Word of God and desperately desires followers of Jesus to discover the power held within it.

Printed in the USA
CPSIA information can be obtained
at www.ICGtesting.com
LVHW040956031223
765241LV00070B/2202